Analytic Anonymity Revisited

Cleaning Out the Freudian Closet

Edited by Neal Spira, MD

Analytic Anonymity Revisited

Cleaning Out the Freudian Closet

Edited by
Neal Spira,
MD

IPBOOKS.net

International Psychoanalytic Books (IPBooks)
New York • www.IPBooks.net

CONTENTS

Introduction

Neal Spira

Does "classical" Freudian technique make it harder to be truly helpful to our patients?

That's the question posed by Henry Friedman in the essay that anchors this volume. Dr. Friedman asserts that the traditional technical posture of "anonymity," rooted in a one-person psychoanalytic worldview, interferes with the healing potential of "give and take" in the psychoanalytic relationship. He suggests that even with our enhanced awareness of the intersubjective nature of that relationship, we tend to remain trapped in a technique that is rooted in anachronistic ideas that make genuine connection more difficult.

In Friedman's view, the use of "classical" language and technique, especially with regard to anonymity, perpetuates a power differential that profoundly impacts on the nature of the relationship and the possibilities it provides for healing. He extends his inquiry into the nature of the relationships we establish with each other in our own professional communities. Anonymity, he argues, is a psychoanalytic concept that should be retired.

Dr. Friedman's paper begets another, implicit question. What would be left of psychoanalytic theory and technique if we got rid of Freud? Can there be a psychoanalysis without core Freudian concepts like transference, resistance and the unconscious? While Friedman emphasizes the implications with regard to psychoanalytic anonymity, our other contributors have widened the scope and, by so doing, try to shed some light on where we're at these days in terms of theory, technique, and the way we employ them—not only in clinical practice, but in our engagement with the greater scientific community.

Among our respondents to Henry's essay, we've invited an eclectic group who speak to the issue from a variety of perspectives. Bhaskar Sripada provides us with a scientific and historical context relevant to the questions Henry poses about contemporary psychoanalytic technique. Lance Dodes approaches the question from the position of a seasoned clinician using theory according to the nuances of each patient-analyst situation. Deana Schuplin addresses the dialectic nature of psychoanalytic theory. Edward Neressian, coming from a neuroscience informed position, highlights the incongruities between classical theory and current knowledge about how the brain works that buttress Henry's arguments from the point of view of our relationship with the scientific community. Dale Gody speaks as a relational psychoanalyst who has come a long way down the road to actualizing what Henry is recommending. And Himanshu Agrawal brings the perspective of a contemporary psychoanalytic candidate.

I hope you enjoy working your way through the varied ways that our contributors approach the issue, and that this volume stimulates your own thinking about where the therapeutic action is in today's psychoanalysis.

Chapter 1
The Problem with Psychoanalytic Anonymity: The Obstacles Created by the Persistence of Traditional Technique

Henry J. Friedman

Because of its unique history psychoanalysis has, to a large measure, remained under the influence of Freud's theoretical and technical vision of what constituted psychoanalysis. His ideas about the unconscious as the repository of both repressed early life experience, as well as of instinctual drives that continue to influence the individual without his or her awareness, were fundamental to his thinking. In order to access the unconscious, he laid down rules about the analyst's technique that included that he the analyst remain neutral, abstinent, and anonymous. Anonymity was important in order for the patient to project onto him aspects of their unconscious past, its drives in the form of wishes; Oedipal wishes, in particular, being seen and privileged as of central importance to the success of any analysis. Analytic theorists who followed Freud attempted to maintain loyalty to his ideas even when they added concepts to theory that were designed to replace his emphasis on the Oedipal phase. Melanie Klein launched an entire body of theory that broadened what Freud had proposed to include the pre-verbal early years of life, which he had specifically declared outside the scope of psychoanalysis as a therapy. Namely, Klein intended by placing emphasis on the infant's mind during the first year of life to include the major psychosis in her explanatory theoretical position; the paranoid-schizoid and depressive phases allowed Klein and her followers to include major psychotic disorders, what we would now call the Axis I illnesses, in the form of something basic to the human mind as it develops. The appeal of Klein's theories to large parts of the analytic world speaks for itself as to the enduring popularity of Klein's ideas, particularly the existence of a psychotic core in all individuals and the importance of the development from the paranoid position to the depressive position. The triumph of Kleinian theory, in either its original iteration or as modified by her followers such as Bion, is more easy to observe than it is to explain. The history of psychoanalytic theory and the direction it has moved in has received little in the way of explanation as to why Freud's theory has fared so poorly in much of the world where major modifications of his theory have prevailed. The answer to this question may well have to do with the requirements of the technique which Freud prescribed as necessary to apply his theory with any patient in traditional psychoanalysis.

At the center of Freud's triad of technical suggestions (actually demands) is the analyst's anonymity, his or her neutrality as in the absence of judgmental responses, and abstinence when it comes to transference gratifications. The constrictions imposed by the analyst who adhered to these rules on himself were clearly manifest in the ego psychology version of psychoanalysis that came to dominate North American psychoanalysts, particularly in the hands of psychiatrist-psychoanalysts, who found the more scientific appearing aspect of ego psychology compatible with a doctor patient relationship, one that fit the medical model and, as such, convinced both analyst and patient of a conventionally acceptable form of treatment. The simplicity of the directions, routinely given by the analyst to his or her patient, initiated a process that was designed to have phases, a beginning or initial, middle, and final or termination phase of the analysis. Once instructed to lay on the couch, four or five times a week, the patient was told to say everything that came to mind, omitting nothing, no matter how seemingly aggressive or sexual, and potentially embarrassing to either the patient or the analyst. The importance of free association was enshrined in Kris's book, *Free Association: Method and Process,* which in itself justified the primacy of free association as giving access to the unconscious mind, where breaks in the associations or connections between a stream of associations was seen as the analyst's tool for uncovering what lay below the surface of rationality that, without the couch and free association, would remain the patient's anchor in unhelpful talk about his or her life based upon his conscious mind. The couch, with the analyst out of the patient's sight, coupled with the demand of saying everything, would undo the dominance of the conscious mind with its ability to filter out the raw instincts of irrationality that were believed to be casual in producing symptoms and affects in the patient's life. Paul Myerson, a traditional ego psychological analyst, wrote *Childhood Dialogues and the Lifting of Repression: Character Structure and Psychoanalytic Technique* in which he defined the goal of psychoanalysis as helping the patient make contact with his or her drives in the sphere of aggression and sexuality, something that he believed would be much more difficult or improbable if the patient's parents had failed to be verbally communicative and non-authoritarian when talking to him as a young child.

Some version of ego psychology dominated in the United States for many decades, successfully keeping competing theoretical schools at bay until it no longer was able to keep control over theory. The degree of domination that it managed to maintain was in itself ultimately the reason for its decline. The work of Charles Brenner and Jacob Arlow enshrined the structural hypothesis with its neat division of the mind into three parts, the ego, the id, and the super-ego, all of which were involved in managing the balance between drives and defense. Anna Freud's *The Ego and the Mechanisms of Defense* served as a manual of defenses which were elaborated and expanded by many ego psychologists. A therapeutic result was attributed to the realization of Freud's dictum that ego now was where the id previously had been; the drives would be mitigated or tamed by insight into their existence which had previously been denied by the individual who was in their grip. In Paul Grey's version of ego psychology, later elaborated by Fred Busch in many articles and books, the analyst was placed in the position, not so much as he or she who knew the answers, but as a careful worker observing the associations moving in front of him, until some aspect of the unconscious could be spotted and called to the patient's attention. Busch added the perspective that the patient's anxiety about deeper material beginning to emerge could only be mined if the analyst tuned in when the patient was in the "neighborhood." By this he meant that the patient had explored enough to be open to seeing deeper drive based material.

The theory of ego psychology was particularly suited to a continuation of classical technique. It resulted in a very silent psychoanalyst, one who was seldom heard, but when he did speak it was to encourage more free association or to render an interpretation of a long stream of associations in the hour, or a connection between associations from any previous hour and the present one. The analyst was saved from the position of being the all-knowing interpreter of the patient's unconscious, a position that risked the accusation of omnipotence from both the patient and from himself. Instead, he became the purveyor of analytic proof, a proof that resided in the ability to demonstrate to the patient that what he interpreted could be proven by examining the patient's associations that proved the correctness of the analyst's interpretation. Dale Boesky, among other classical ego psychologists, wrote extensively about what he called "psychoanalytic proof." The analyst, as a person, was safe from participation in what was assumed to be a particularly intimate dyadic relationship, one in which the transference and counter-transference became increasingly the source of rich material, in dreams and associations, that contained important passions, both sexual and aggressive in nature. This assumption, however, ignored the fact that the intimacy was one sided; the patient revealed everything about himself while the analyst remained anonymous. He participated from behind a professional safe, anonymous self. He did participate by his interpretations but his feelings were to be seen as countertransference and, as such, needed to be contained, split off, for his own consideration, but not to be shared with the patient.

External reality was widely seen as irrelevant or even more likely the enemy of a true analysis. Hence, patients in a crisis, acute or chronic, were seen as not suitable for a continuing analysis of intra-psychic conflict; the very thing, or the only thing, that really allowed a patient to be an analysand in the true sense of the concept. Any analytic treatment where the reality of the patient's life issues didn't fade into the background could be seen as a failure of selection; the analyst had simply taken the wrong type of patient into analysis. If an analysis was working the patient's thoughts, wishes, and drives would be focused on the analyst. Weekends, in particular, were seen as an interruption in the patient's relationship to the analyst with the result that many things that occurred over a weekend were interpreted or brought back to the impact of the interruption. The analyst's vacations or interruptions for illness or family demands became the focus of analytic hours leading up to the break, and then analyzed after the break. The search for the intra-psychic conflicts as the exclusive arena for psychoanalysis was from a very early point in the growth of analysis in the United States opposed by Harry Stack Sullivan and Clara Thompson, who strongly believed that the nature of the environment that a patient developed in greatly influenced the problems in living that each patient experienced in adult life. The child was, in the eyes of the inter-personal school of analysts, programed to react in patterned ways that had been part of the family culture. The behavior of the parents explained much that one could see in the patients that they analyzed. This assertion of difference cost the interpersonal school analysts a great deal. They were simply exiled from the American Psychoanalytic Association, literally driven out of a national meeting having been stripped of their membership. After being driven out of the APsaA they grouped together to form the William Alanson White Institute, a New York phenomenon, that provided a home for likeminded psychoanalysts, many of whom were psychologists rather than psychiatrists.

The interpersonal perspective morphed into the relational approach and, in doing so, began to create an approach to patients that differed significantly from the ego psychological perspective. However, they did so without specifying any change in technique other than to see their patients at a three-times-per-week frequency and have them sitting up instead of lying on a couch. While their theoretical differences combined with these two technical changes implied a different position for the psychoanalyst, they remained tied to the terms transference and counter-transference, implying the continued acceptance of analysis as not including a real relationship. Even allowing for the influence of a face-to-face position, there is little to indicate where the relational school stands with regard to the important issue of self-disclosure on the analyst's part. For that matter, the relational school left much of the traditional approach apparently in place, instead emphasizing the concept of enactment. By this they are referring to something that happens between analyst and patient that is only observed and analyzed after it has taken place. It has a kind of "eureka" feel to it when the analyst recognizes that he has been participating in enacting a role in the patient's unconscious or patterned behavior that he has been unaware of. The implication of this emphasis on enactments within the relational approach is that the analyst has, in some fashion, been more active, more of a participant and then an observer, rather than a participant-observer as in the interpersonal perspective. The analyst through his activity has failed to remain a detached and neutral participant in the dyadic relationship. However, in relational circles, this is seen not as the result of a failure of technique, but rather an inevitable outcome of the analyst's willingness to participate in some more active a fashion than was traditionally considered permissible.

Self-disclosure has been a touchstone in the rather tortured approach to openness on the analyst's part about who they are and what they feel about life and about their patients. Among traditional analysts in the United States, it has been viewed as a failure on the analyst's part; an indication that his training analysis failed to help him master the capacity for anonymity, abstinence and neutrality, producing an incomplete psychoanalyst still too inclined to be involved with his patient as a real person. If seen from a certain progressive perspective many aspects of classical psychoanalytic technique have been designed to create a functional dyadic relationship that is almost entirely impersonal in nature where the analyst is concerned. If the details of the analyst's background or his political views or religious observation or non-observation have been disclosed, or enter into the analytic dialogue, it has been assumed that this will truncate the development of the supposedly necessary "transference neurosis." Like many of the received wisdoms of psychoanalysis in the Freudian tradition, little has been subject to questioning, no less revision, or retirement of the concept. The fear of self-disclosure has continued to dominate not just those who are psychoanalytically trained and oriented. Therapists of many different schools continue to accept the technical rule of anonymity despite being CBT or DBT specialists. The power of psychoanalytic rules for technique cannot be overestimated simply because it has only been in psychoanalysis that such rules have been promulgated and maintained as established without any proof, experimentally or clinically, to prove their importance or their effectiveness.

The desire for an impersonal but nevertheless intimate and intense relationship between psychoanalyst and patient has its roots in a number of issues that have occurred during many decades of psychoanalytic practice. The concept of the "erotic transference" as a common and perhaps inevitable outcome of having a female patient on the couch with a male psychoanalyst behind that couch somehow was accepted as an established reality without any consideration of how frequently such a transference did appear and consideration of what the diagnosis of the patients who developed such a sexualized love for her analyst actually was. Once the idea of transference took hold in the psychoanalytic world, the existence of an erotic transference as an inevitability was accepted as bedrock; it was an entity that wasn't to be questioned. As a result, it was often looked for and found by psychoanalysts of varying perspectives, and even being seen as a hallmark of heterosexuality in a female patient. It's absence needed to be understood as representing something missing in the analysis of a woman patient by a male analyst. Less was said about the situation, transference wise, when the patient was male with a female analyst but basically a similar transference was felt to be inevitable. It is likely that the erotic transference did become a lively and disruptive feature when the patient was a woman with the type of instability that we characterize as typical of borderline personality disordered patients. Such patients, as a result of their loose boundaries, were seen as proof of the existence and importance of the erotic transference. This sometimes did result in actual sexual activity between such a patient and a male analyst who himself had an absence of needed boundaries, with the result of a sexually passionate relationship that somehow always had a bad outcome for both patient and analyst.

However, the majority of sexual romances between analyst and patient tended to be between a male analyst and a female candidate who was in analysis as part of her training. While the profession condemned such relationships and labeled them as acting out between a poorly trained analyst and a seducible female candidate, it is plausible to consider these relationships as rather like the affairs that sometimes occur when a married man meets and falls into a relationship with a desirable woman. The fear of such an occurrence within the psychoanalytic profession has been a major contribution to supporting the need for a distance between patient and analyst. Self-disclosure was viewed as the beginning of what could become a "slippery slope" that would result in a dangerous degree of relatedness between and within the analytic dyad. In order to preserve the analyzing function of the analyst, it was deemed necessary that both participants managed to minimize their actual relationship as two participating adults. The erotic transference, when accepted as a given, has contributed to the demand for adherence to technical practices that keep psychoanalysis distant from the personal with regard to both the patient and analyst. However, it is the analyst who is officially entitled to concealment of most, if not all, details of their personal and emotional life. Added to this is the tendency for the analyst to work from behind a professional self, one that conceals his feelings about himself, his work, life in general, in order to preserve his analyzing function.

The original model of psychoanalysis defined access to the drive-derivatives in the form of wishes as its goal. The lifting of repression that kept the infantile out of consciousness justified a strict adherence to neutrality, anonymity and abstinence on the analyst's part. The person of the analyst, his special proclivities as an individual, his politics, his esthetics were his to show in his personal life but not during his functioning as a psychoanalyst. The journalist Janet Malcolm in her book, *The Impossible Profession,* created a picture of a typical psychoanalyst that vividly described the analyst of that period with his plain office, the absence of any original art (just reproductions of well-known paintings), as well as any photographs of family members, maybe a portrait of Freud and of course a simple couch, an analytic couch that resembled a day bed. The analyst himself was conservatively dressed with a suit and tie, sometimes a vest, he was permitted to smoke while taking copious, often verbatim notes on the patient's associations and his interpretations, if and when he felt it important to intrude upon the patient's free associations to render an interpretation. It was considered best for interpretations to be spare and concise in order to make an impact upon the patient, certainly nothing like a conversational rhythm or tone was to be present.

For many analysts the requirements of technique were comfortable and for some even exactly matched to their personalities. Seriousness, even carried to a point of dourness, seemed to be the personality style of many who were drawn to psychoanalysis. It was a time of conventionality, where family values and a dignified style in those selected to be candidates in training were searched for by institutes of the American Psychoanalytic Association. If by practice, rather than overt rule, all homosexual psychiatrists were considered unanalyzable and unsuitable for psychoanalytic training. Divorce was an anathema because it revealed that a candidate wasn't capable of object constancy or that he failed to recognize that his anger at his wife actually was a derivative of his unanalyzed relationship to his mother. A tight control of who, after graduation, could be elevated to a training analyst position insured that the elite analysts would constitute the Institute, the important part where decisions about candidates and education were made, while the remaining, less elevated analysts would form the Society of that particular institute. By maintaining such a model, each institute could guarantee the continuity of the culture of that institute. The training analyst committee consisting of training analysts only would select graduate analysts who they felt were worthy of being considered for elevation to TA. Even then these candidates would be screened, interviewed, and all the TAs questioned about the acceptability of that now invited applicant. If any powerful TA objected to the person being considered it was likely that elevation to TA would be impossible for that individual. The number of TAs was kept small enough for each

TA to have a sizable number of candidates on their couch; this made it possible for the TAs to have a secure income as most training analyses lasted well over five years.

The effectiveness of this organizational system was undeniable; most important was the ability of the training analyst group at any local institute to reproduce itself. Since graduates could only apply when "tapped" or selected to be considered by the TAs, other talented individual analysts could be ignored. As a result, the TA establishment essentially reproduced itself with great reliability. This meant that, whether wittingly or not, only those analysts whose personality fit with the established group were asked to join. Of course, mistakes were made, particularly when an analyst had written an impressive paper or more, but once elevated to TA status most of these individuals quickly learned to fall in line and not rock the boat by being outspoken about any controversial issue. The stability of successful institutes like the Boston Psychoanalytic Society and Institute (BPSI) and the New York Psychoanalytic Institute (NYPI) were impressive, although they differed from each other probably on the basis of contrast in Boston types (proper and unassuming) as opposed to New York types (aggressive and outspoken) of personalities.

The harmony among the TA group did begin to break down probably because of a number of factors. First, in Boston, for instance, those analysts who had been considered for elevation to TA but turned down began to protest that the TA selection committee included no non-TA members. This was a period in the United States when the absolute nature of all hierarchies was being questioned. Students at major universities were demanding to be included on committees that concerned their future as well as that of the university. The response at BPSI was dramatic; a group of TAs were so angered by the insistence that there should be non-TAs on the committee they proposed leaving BPSI to form a new psychoanalytic institute in Boston. Despite the fact that Boston was a rather small city the APsaA approved PINE as a new entity in Boston. In addition, the dwindling number of psychiatric residents applying for training that followed a shift in psychiatric training to a more psycho-biological orientation directed young psychiatrists away from analytic psychotherapy. The compromise settlement of a lawsuit by three psychologists opened psychoanalytic training to psychologists and eventually this was extended to include social workers. The lessening of a medical approach in turn reduced the influence of ego psychology in general as other approaches advocated by Klein, Bion, Kohut and Lacan combined to influence how psychoanalysis was taught in both the institutes affiliated with the APsaA, as well as those independent institutes that were established after the lawsuit was settled.

The growth of psychoanalytic theory has resulted in a more fragmented field not only with regard to competing theories but in terms of a tendency to "pick and choose" from among theories that are, in themselves, incompatible. Furthermore, as psychiatric residents have increasingly avoided training in psychoanalysis the field has been populated by individuals who, although well trained in psychology and social work, are far removed from the practical demands of medicine that require continuing monitoring for effectiveness of any treatment. Psychoanalysis in the hands of those who know only psychoanalytic theory without reference to pragmatic measures of relief and progress in their patients' lives can easily become entrapped in the view that the theory they believe in is correct and effective, no matter what their patients report about how they are doing. This is vividly illustrated by the work of several Italian psychoanalysts who have enveloped their work in the theories of Bion and Winnicott. Antonio Ferro, for instance, insists that anything other than what happens in the analytic hour should be of no importance to the analyst. In his colorful version of psychoanalysis, the only thing that is, in his language of the kitchen, "cooking" is in the relationship between the analyst and his patient. He reduces the patient's life to a kind of irrelevant position, as in, "the patient says she has a dog, but how do I know if she does," meaning that he doesn't care about the details of the patient's life. Here, in Ferro, is an example of psychoanalytic reductionism taken to a degree where only the transference-countertransference interaction has meaning that is worth the effort of interpretation.

Traditional psychoanalysis flourished in New York City where the New York Psychoanalytic Institute following analysts like Charles Brenner and Jacob Arlow codified the structural hypothesis as the very center of psychoanalysis. Their efforts were directed at defining psychoanalysis as a scientifically based therapy that aimed at discovering the causal aspects of human development, as well as human emotional conflict and suffering. By elevating the dual drive hypothesis, they defined psychoanalysis as accounting for all aspects of development. The libidinal and aggressive drives on encountering the defenses against allowing direct expression of the drives resulted in what they called compromise formations. All of human development was seen as a compromise formation and the same was said of all interpersonal interactions. Compromise formation was the center of this infantile drive-defense model. Within this perspective every aspect of the developing individual had to be viewed as the result of a compromise formation, with a resultant product that could be deconstructed to its component parts. The interaction of the drives with the relevant defenses, both of which were largely unconscious, resulted in what could be observed about any individual's sexual and aggressive characteristics.

This model placed the psychoanalyst in the position of knowing what was really occurring with a patient no matter how much the patient found an interpretation to be wrong, irrelevant, or harmful. Furthermore, this role, which was at the center of ego psychology, the analytic approach that gained almost complete acceptance and dominance in the U.S. and North America, reinforced the idea of technical excellence built around anonymity, abstinence and neutrality. The character and personality of the analyst, in this vision of psychoanalysis was not only irrelevant but a danger to a therapy remaining in the realm of what could be properly called psychoanalysis. The demands on the analyst to remain a listening and interpreting object were seen as a kind of badge of courage. The enduring analyst was one who could keep themselves and their emotions out of the field even at great sacrifice to themselves of human involvement in the lives of their patients. A true psychoanalyst could, in their personal life, be lively, funny, compassionate, a great colleague, and friend, but all of this was to disappear when in his or her professional role as listener for and interpreter of the unconscious. While it is popular now to deny that this could ever be what we as psychoanalysts believed was at the core of our functioning, it remains true that it did exist as a view and that view has continued to influence analysts to work from an anonymous position. While this attitude towards revealing one's personal history and life to patients during the course of an analysis is claimed by contemporary conflict theory analysts to not continue to be the case, there is much evidence that it continues to influence many, if not most, psychoanalysts in the United States as well as in the rest of the world. From this perspective no self-disclosure should be part of a routine analysis. If it did unfortunately occur, it was necessary that the analyst be able to justify such an occurrence on the basis of the unconscious relationship within the dyad at the particular moment of self-disclosure.

The anonymous analyst in all of the traditional schools of analysis meant that you, as the analyst, was the serious, functional adult in the consulting room. Analysts were to be seen as serious individuals who remained dedicated to the task of analyzing the intra-psychic conflicts of their patients. The patient on the couch was asked to regress and believed to be like a child in a parent (analyst), child (patient), relationship. The analysts needed to carefully protect themselves in their personal lives or, as depicted in the movie, "What about Bob," the patient might be expected to invade your life by acting out their fascination with the analyst's life. The desire of a patient to literally become totally focused on the analyst's life, his choices and his preferences was seen as an inevitable problem if the analyst responded to the patient's curiosity by answering questions about his personal life. The infantile unconscious was seen as insatiable once a transference neurosis has taken hold within the analytic dyad.

Because there are some patients with inadequate character structures to maintain a separation between a real therapeutic relationship when it allows the analyst to be known as a person with specific other relationships in his life, it has led to the conclusion that this is a danger with all patients in analysis. Clinicians who have been burnt by patients with borderline personality disorders, patients who respond with intense, erotic and aggressive involvements with the analyst, have contributed to making anonymity, or at least mostly remaining anonymous, seem essential if an analysis isn't to be derailed or "blown up" by the unworkable aspects of analysis with such individuals. When a patient develops affects of erotic love or murderous hate along with the insistence that these feelings are justified by some aspect of the analyst's perceived action, the situation becomes clinically untenable. In addition, it reinforces the received assertion (wisdom) that analysis is a dangerous endeavor simply because, to be successful it must reach those deeply buried parts of the infantile self that had remained unconscious and bound through repression in all individuals (patients).

If the interdiction against self-disclosure is dropped along with the insistence on neutrality and abstinence, what kind of participation by the analyst should be expected if the therapeutic goals of an analysis are to be enhanced? The traditional austere analyst who was motivated by the desire to undo repression, and in doing so help the patient gain access to their infantile core self, could feel secure in their task because it was so clearly defined and delimited. By maintaining technical requirements, the theory upon which traditional psychoanalysis was based could remain unquestioned. The effort for all theoretical schools to maintain the basic rules of technique has resulted in an absence of models for the analyst's activity, other than interpretation, during the course of an analysis. While much has been made of changes in psychoanalysis in the direction of changing it into a two-person relationship, such claims seem to exist more in their assertion than in the reality of actual practice.

The position of many if not most analysts continues to regard a "real" relationship between analyst and patient in terms of transference and countertransference. These terms are more than mere words when it comes to the encounter between an adult patient who is seeking help for problems and or symptoms of anxiety and depression and an adult psychoanalyst or analytic psychotherapist. Are these two strangers, connected as they are by a professional relationship, not really encountering each other and reacting in accordance to what is real between them? Merton Gill alerted us to the idea that, while everything was transference, nevertheless the perception of the patient regarding the analyst might well be grounded in something real about the analyst. Joseph Lichtenberg suggested that the analyst wear the attributions made about him as if they were real. But, the desire to place the source of an affective response to the analyst on past figures in the patient's life persists. Jane Hall in a recent email exchange attempted to convince me that if a male patient in his twenties felt that I was judging him for his sexual hyperactivity it was probable that the disapproval belonged with his puritanical father. She put this forward as proof that it is always transference, to which, I would say, no, in fact I did disapprove of his indifference to the feelings of the other in a sexual encounter.

Analysts are creatures of habit and often prisoners of theory and basic assumptions. If a new relationship between patient and therapist is supposed to have no basis for emotional reaction because the analyst remains anonymous and therefore cannot have elicited an angry or sexual response when one does occur, habit makes the therapist look to a past figure rather than to themselves. To think outside the habitual framework of feelings in the patient or in the analyst that requires it be seen as a transference or a counter-transference depends upon a certain braveness of spirit in the analyst. If we consider and acknowledge that most training in psychoanalysis doesn't encourage thinking that is critical of received wisdom about either the theory of that institute and certainly not the importance of technical rules, then it becomes clear that a two-person psychoanalysis and adherence to categorizing feelings in the patient or analyst as transference and countertransference is an impossibility. The patient is asked to be completely open, to say everything that comes to mind, to conceal nothing from the analyst, who, on the other hand, is given the privilege and responsibility of remaining anonymous. The power of the anonymous analyst cannot be overestimated. He or she by remaining anonymous gains from a mysteriousness that implies an all knowing or magical persona. This power has proven difficult to give up; to be known in one's actual personality and life is to risk being judged as anything, ranging from nothing special to something that is disapproved of by the patient.

Are you observant of a religion, particularly if the analyst has a Jewish background and the patient is an observant Jew or a Christian, who believes that Jews should be observant? Are you married or divorced? Are you straight or gay? Do you back the democratically-elected President? All of these knotty issues that we all, as therapists, have as positions in our personal life can be hidden from our patients with the rationalization that it is a necessity if a transference neurosis is going to emerge. The price of protecting the transference from being invaded by the reality of the psychoanalyst's personal life and character is to keep the analysis a one-person endeavor. The apparent two-person nature achieved by allowing the analyst to utilize his countertransference responses represents a pseudo two-person entity; it looks like two persons but it is, in actuality, two unconscious entities interacting, with the analyst claiming to himself and to the patient, the accuracy of his interpretation of the patient's transference, as well as his correct reading of his own countertransference. To say that there is no real give-and-take or conversation between two adults in an analysis conducted on this basis is an understatement. It perhaps helps us understand the frequent observation, when talking to individuals who have had a traditional psychoanalysis, that what they recall about what was important to them in their experience of their analyst lies in how they recall and describe some small moment of unexpected human exchange with the analyst.

What guidelines are there for any analyst who decides that his role shouldn't be restricted to that of a receptive listener who interprets his patient's associations but remains outside of a personal relationship between himself and his patient? Gabbard, quoting Bion says: "The analyst you become is you and you alone, you have to respect the uniqueness of your own personality—that is what you use, not all these interpretations (these theories that you use to combat the feeling that you are not really an analyst and do not know how to become one)."

However, there is little evidence that in his clinical work Bion actually revealed much if anything about his personal life or his non-professional personality. Gabbard goes further towards defining a more liberated psychoanalyst when he states the following: In 2009 Gabbard and Ogden (On becoming a psychoanalyst, *Int J Psa* 90:311–327) wrote that "Each time we start an analysis, we have an obligation and responsibility to become an analyst whom we have never been before. This requires that we drop the script and enter into a conversation of a type we have never before experienced."

But, a great deal is left unsaid as to what dropping the script and entering into a conversation that is unique to each patient will involve or look like. On the surface, Gabbard and Ogden are saying something profound that expresses exactly what I am aiming at in this paper but without spelling out how difficult it is for most analysts to overcome the rules that they were taught as essential to being a psychoanalyst. The past, to paraphrase Faulkner, isn't actually dead, it isn't even past. While it would be appealing to accept the ubiquitous insistence that "we are no longer like that" in regard to our silence and absence of open participation of our actual life and inner state in the analytic dyad, the truth is that this seems more a wished for state of our field than an actual reflection of how much the past still dominates even from the undercover and disguise that denial provides.

Once an analyst concludes that the basis for all our theories are indeed theoretical and unable to be either disproven or proven, it is possible to face the need to be real with his patients. Without active input and participation from the analyst, it is unlikely that many crucial subjects will be introduced into the dialogue by the patient. In a recent paper, Dorothy Holmes introduced the idea that all analysts should introduce the subject of the patient's probable, or as she sees it, inevitable, racism to the analysis. She is aware of race because as a black woman psychoanalyst she is keenly aware that race can never be a subject that fails to enter the analyses that she conducts. The same can be said for all of us who accept the basic two-person nature of the relationship; contrary to the old rules of anonymity it is crucial to a relation-based analysis that the analyst include and introduce much material that comes from his own life experience and subjective emotional response to events that surround us regardless of the degree to which we involve ourselves in current events, political crises, and mortality. The gradient of the traditional psychoanalytic relationship in which the analyst alone has knowledge of the unconscious aspects of the patient's mind, while keeping track of his own unconscious fantasies and responses, leaves the patient with a residue of an empowered and omnipotent analyst who is to remain unknown as a real person. The changes in the analytic relationship that occur when the analyst allows himself the freedom to participate in an active role serve as a corrective to many of the deficits that are readily apparent in traditional psychoanalytic treatments. In terms of therapeutic action, the presence of the analyst as a real and continuing influence on the patient's capacity to maintain the growth that has occurred during the analysis far exceeds what has been the case after the termination with a traditionally anonymous analyst.

Chapter 2
Neutrality, Abstinence, and Anonymity: From an Objective Observer Towards an Active-Participant Observer

Bhaskar Sripada

Introduction

A century after its establishment, psychoanalysis remains a young field, with analysts grappling to solidify its theoretical, scientific, and clinical underpinnings while drawing lessons from their experiences and mistakes. This paper responds to Friedman's work, "The Problem with Psychoanalytic Anonymity: The Obstacles Created by The Persistence of Traditional Technique." This paper will also examine how neutrality, abstinence, and anonymity relate to objectivity and the historical and contemporary scientific influences shaping psychoanalysis.

Reactions to Friedman's essay

In his paper on neutrality, abstinence, and anonymity, Friedman delves into the insights of psychoanalytic pioneers, underscores critical theories, engages in the ongoing debate about whether psychoanalysis aligns more with a one-person or two-person psychology, discusses the nuances of Transference and countertransference, and scrutinizes the dynamics and controversies surrounding the Training Analyst system. Considering the vastness of the subject matter, Friedman's exposition is sometimes impressionistic, even lyrical. I aim to distill some of Friedman's primary arguments along with my commentary.

Concerning psychoanalytic technique, Friedman notes, "At the core of Freud's triad of technical suggestions (effectively demands) is the analyst's anonymity, neutrality devoid of judgmental responses, and abstinence from transference gratifications." Analysts traditionally operated under the assumption that adherence to principles such as practice, neutrality, abstinence, and anonymity enabled them to serve as objective and privileged observers. This implied that the analyst's personality remained detached from the analytic process, and their interpretations aimed to address patient conflicts through an accurate understanding of the patient's reality.

Friedman (2020) underscores the real and tangible presence of the analyst in any analysis within these interpersonal and intersubjective contexts. The central argument put forth by Friedman revolves around the notion that, despite claims of substantial deviations from Freud's instinct-Oedipus complex model of psychoanalysis, the disagreements between traditional and contemporary psychoanalytic schools primarily exist on a theoretical level. In practical terms, many contemporary psychoanalytic schools still adhere to some form of the traditional psychoanalytic approach involving neutrality, abstinence, and anonymity.

Harry Stack Sullivan and Clara Thompson asserted that an individual's developmental environment plays a significant role in shaping them, introducing the concept of interpersonal psychology. Within this framework, they acknowledged the vital role of enactments in life and the analytic setting. Interpersonal psychology, which laid the foundation for two-person psychology, highlighted the active participation of both individuals in a relationship. They acknowledged that the analyst is either an active participant or a participant observer, making pure objectivity unattainable.

Friedman contends that the "price of protecting the Transference from being invaded by the reality of the psychoanalyst's personal life and character is to keep the analysis a one-person endeavor. The apparent two-person nature achieved by allowing the analyst to utilize his countertransference responses represents a pseudo-two-person entity; it looks like two persons, but it is, in actuality, two unconscious entities interacting with the analyst claiming to himself and to the patient the accuracy of his interpretation of the patient's transference, as well as his correct reading of his own countertransference."

In this context, Friedman asserts that within contemporary psychoanalysis, despite the analyst appearing to engage in a two-person dynamic by recognizing and incorporating countertransference responses, the analysis fundamentally operates as a pseudo-two-person entity. The essential argument is that, in practice, it sustains a one-person psychology framework. The analyst maintains a privileged position, interfacing with the patient's unconscious, affirming the precision of interpretations, and simultaneously upholding a degree of neutrality, anonymity, and detachment from the patient.

Friedman highlights that while Freud's Oedipal theories center on the psychology of post-infant childhood, Melanie Klein introduced an extensive theoretical framework that broadened Freud's concepts to include the pre-verbal early years of life—a period explicitly excluded by Freud from the scope of psychoanalysis. Klein emphasized the mental development of infants during their first year, exploring the paranoid-schizoid and depressive phases. This expansion enabled Klein and her followers to engage in psychoanalytic speculations about major psychotic disorders. Despite these theoretical differences, Friedman notes that Kleinian psychology remained aligned with the technique prescribed by Freud.

Similarly, Brenner and Arlow, operating within the framework of Ego psychology, defined psychoanalysis as a scientifically grounded therapy. They focused on uncovering the causal factors of human development and emotional conflict, highlighting the significance of compromise formations (Arlow and Brenner,1964; Brenner, 1994). However, according to Friedman, these advancements did not significantly impact the notions of the analyst's anonymity. Instead, they further solidified the concept of the anonymous, neutral "very silent psychoanalyst."

According to Friedman, "External reality was widely seen as irrelevant or even more likely the enemy of a true analysis. Hence, patients in a crisis, acute or chronic, were seen as not suitable for a continuing analysis of intra-psychic conflict, the very thing, or the only thing that really allowed a patient to be an analysand in the true sense of the concept. Any analytic treatment where the reality of the patient's life issues didn't fade into the background could be seen as a failure of selection; the analyst had simply taken the wrong type of patient into analysis. If an analysis was working the patient's thoughts, wishes and drives would be focused on the analyst."

The idea of an external reality suggests that there is also an internal reality. This distinction between the inner and outer world is acknowledged by many analysts, who recognize the differences between the intrapsychic and interpersonal domains. Throughout history, the distinction between external and internal realities has been the subject of much philosophical debate and disagreement. One way to comprehend this distinction is to compare the philosophical perspectives of naive realism and indirect (active-observer-dependent) realism, two different approaches to understanding reality. Naive realists assert a clear separation between external and internal reality, while indirect realists question the feasibility of such a straightforward separation.

In this essay, Friedman implies that the analyst's unconscious grandiosity or the fear of an erotic transference or countertransference might explain the continued adherence to neutrality, abstinence, and anonymity in contemporary psychoanalysis. He suggests that psychoanalysts, believing in their inherent understanding of a patient's situation, maintain a conviction that they know the true nature of the analysis, regardless of the patient's disagreement with interpretations. Friedman points out that this attitude risks the analyst assuming "omnipotence" within the analytic setting.

Friedman explores the relationship between neutral, abstinent, and anonymous analysts and the dangers of self-disclosure leading to the risks of a "slippery slope" to an erotic transference or countertransference. Concern about enactments has been with psychoanalysis since its early days. In the early years of psychoanalysis, Ferenczi recommended that analysts help patients overcome early emotional deprivation by gratifying their craving for love and affection, including hugging and kissing them. Freud (1931) was concerned that this *kissing technique* would lead to further erotic escalation.

What remedies does Friedman recommend for the persistence of neutrality, abstinence, and anonymity in contemporary psychoanalysis?

Friedman suggests that contemporary psychoanalysts must embrace their uniqueness and creativity rather than adhere to rigid rules and scripts that limit their engagement with each patient. He supports his argument by quoting Gabbard, who draws on Bion's idea that "The analyst you become is you and you alone, you have to respect the uniqueness of your own personality—that is what you use, not all these interpretations (these theories that you use to combat the feeling that you are not really an analyst and do not know how to become one").

Friedman also cites Gabbard and Ogden (2009), who state, "Each time we start an analysis, we have an obligation and responsibility to become an analyst whom we have never been before. This requires that we drop the script and enter into a conversation of a type we have never before experienced."

However, Friedman acknowledges that this is easier said than done and that many analysts struggle to overcome and change ingrained habits and expectations. Friedman concludes, "But, a great deal is left unsaid as to what dropping the script and entering into a conversation that is unique to each patient will involve or look like. On the surface, Gabbard and Ogden are saying something profound that expresses exactly what I am aiming at in this paper but without spelling out how difficult it is for most analysts to overcome the rules that they were taught as essential to being a psychoanalyst. The past, to paraphrase Faulkner, isn't actually dead, it isn't even past."

There are significant differences between traditional psychoanalysis with the assumption of a privileged observer and contemporary psychoanalysis with an active participant observer in two-person psychology. They mirror the conflicts between classical traditional science based on absolutes, objectivity, and Positivism and modern science based on relativity, active observer, and complementarity.

Science, objectivity, neutrality, abstinence, and anonymity

Freud's *Weltanschauung*, or worldview, comprised a single intellectual construction and an explanation of the universe. This all-encompassing ideal hypothesis provided a comprehensive and internally consistent solution to all facets of human existence, grounded in observed phenomena and research, while rejecting revelation or divination as part of its method (Freud, 1933, pp. 170–171).

Freud formulated psychoanalysis in an era dominated by Cartesian dualism and Positivism. Descartes (1628), with his "method of doubt," established a dualistic framework asserting that subjects could objectively measure external objects without influencing them. Comte's (1855) Positivism further emphasized that verified scientific propositions lead to objective truths. These notions, inherent in classical science, significantly influenced early psychoanalytic practitioners.

Not only was the scientific observer assumed to be objective, but Freud believed that the patient could also become an objective collaborator. Freud (1893) said,

"By explaining things to him [the patient], by giving him information about the marvelous world of psychical processes into which we ourselves only gained insight by such analyses, we make him himself into a collaborator, induce him to regard himself with the objective interest of an investigator, and thus push back his resistance."

Furthermore, Freud's (1893) view was that patients can learn... and adopt an attitude of "completely objective observation" towards the psychical processes taking place in them.

Freud, guided by objectivity and Positivism, integrated the principles of neutrality, abstinence, and anonymity into the foundational fabric of psychoanalytic technique. Freud considered these concepts, derived from his overarching worldview and the scientific ethos of his time, as crucial for preserving a rigorous and impartial analytical process. The analyst aimed to maintain a neutral stance to prevent bias or influence on the patient's process. By abstaining from satisfying any transference wishes that might arise, the analyst avoided interfering with the patient's analysis and allowed the unconscious material to emerge. The analyst's anonymity also created a safe space for the patient to project freely without interference from the analyst's personal characteristics or opinions.

In response to these influences, psychoanalysts embraced analytic neutrality, embodying the notion of the blank-screen anonymous analyst. This view held that the analyst should function as a neutral canvas onto which the patient projects conflicts and transferences. Many analysts felt that an objective and neutral analyst was feasible, necessary, and desirable, asserting that professional relationships could remain insulated from personal influences. Due to the analyst's role demanding anonymity, early practitioners deemed it unwise to disclose any personal details. This perspective engendered a technical approach in psychoanalytic practices. Analysts, in their clarifications, interpretations, interventions, and even in matters like billing, payment, vacation, sickness, and gift policies, draped themselves in a veil of neutrality to preserve the metaphorical blank screen.

The sciences underwent revolutionary changes at the start of the twentieth century, rejecting the objective observer, certainty, and the notion of an independent reality. For example, Edelman (1992, pp. 66–68) pointed out that classical science assumes an objective "God's eye view" by denying the observer's mind, consciousness, and intentions. In contrast to the omniscient perspective of classical God's-eye views, modern science explicitly acknowledges that each observer, based on location and personality, holds a specific perspective. Therefore, contemporary generalizations do not result in absolute or universally applicable statements; they are qualified and restricted by specific observations, observational methods, and the observer.

Edelman argues that a scientist's apparatus arrangement affects their measurements and outcomes, leading to modern scientific principles that recognize the active observer's role. Edelman has developed a framework for modern science that considers the active observer's (scientist's) mind, consciousness, and intention.

This abandonment of objectivity mirrors the revolutionary modern science discoveries, such as the study of subatomic events. Heisenberg (1958, p. 50) recognized that, in the subatomic sphere, there is no neutral observer; the scientist invariably influences what he observes, and that exact determination is impossible. Heisenberg discovered that an inevitable and somewhat uncontrolled mutual interaction exists between the observer and the observed. The apparent object under observation is not revealed in its intrinsic state but rather as a combination of the object's properties influenced by the measurements conducted by the observer. Heisenberg's principle states that every observation involves the observer and the object, which are theoretically inseparable. Consequently, a direct and independent observation of a designated object is impossible.

Bohr and Einstein engaged in a disagreement initiated in 1927 at the fifth Solvay Conference among physicists, focusing on their contrasting perspectives regarding the nature of reality. Bohr advocated for the concept of complementarity, positing that particles display wave and particle characteristics based on observation. Bohr asserted that, at the quantum level, entities possess only probabilities until measured.

In contrast, Einstein adhered to scientific realism, asserting that confirmed scientific theories faithfully depict reality. Einstein argued for a deterministic worldview, positing that physical systems possess objective properties independently of observation. He famously stated, "God does not play dice," to express his dissatisfaction with the probabilistic nature of quantum mechanics (Skibba, 2018).

The central dispute revolved around whether the quantum realm was fundamentally probabilistic, as per Bohr's proposal, or whether an independent reality existed, as Einstein believed. This debate held profound philosophical implications for our comprehension of reality, determinism, and the role of observation in shaping the physical world. Bohr's and Heisenberg's perspectives, emphasizing the active observer and embracing a probabilistic nature, have proven extraordinarily successful in elucidating the microscopic world.

There is skepticism towards a naive view of reality in Western and Eastern philosophical traditions. Berkeley, for instance, rejects the notion of material things being independent of the mind or existing as separate substances. Berkeley (Downing, 2021) posits that there are no such mind-independent entities; instead, he famously states that *"esse est percipi (aut percipere)"*—to be is to be perceived (or to perceive).

In his work "Critique of Pure Reason," Kant (1781) posited that space and time are not inherent attributes of the physical world; instead, they constitute elements of the mental framework essential for our experience of the world. Consequently, objects in space and time rely on the mind for their existence. This concept aligns with Kant's notion of the "phenomenal" world, representing the world as it appears to our perception.

Sankara, a philosopher of the seventh century, formalized Vedanta philosophy by positing the concept of Maya, which is the Self projecting its own attributes onto the world (Grimes, 2004). The concept of Maya involves the idea that the world is real, but as a phenomenal reality that depends on the observer. Therefore, we can only experience the world through the veil of our Self-consciousness. This projection of the Self to the world involves concealment (Avarna) and misrepresentation (Viksepa). A typical example explaining Maya is the rope and the snake illusion. When a person sees a rope and mistakes it for a snake, one Avarna hides the true nature of the rope, and Viksepa creates an illusory false image of the snake (Raju, 1953). However, the perception of illusory snakes has causal effects if the person believes in them. Maya implies that the world cannot be separated from the Self and is always a reflection of some part of the Self.

Einstein steadfastly adhered to the concept of an objective and independent reality, a perspective that persists in numerous disciplines. Similarly, some contemporary psychoanalysts continue to practice based on the belief in the analyst's objectivity and neutrality. Schwaber (2005), for instance, emphasized this perspective, stating, "I felt secure in the knowledge that I had set aside my personal feelings, preserving my analytic neutrality."

The resistance to the complete application of the idea of an active participant observer does not apply to analysts such as Schwaber. However, as Friedman notes in this paper, it does apply to many contemporary analysts who profess two-person psychology and the active observer and persist in notions of neutrality. For example, Galatzer-Levy (1991) states, "Self-psychology largely continues in a mode of naïve realism about entities like self, self object, and mind despite careful commentary that suggests more sophisticated positions."

Wisdom drawn from atomic sciences and the accumulated insights from decades of analytic work suggests that in psychoanalysis as well, the observer plays an active role. Therefore, analysts must overcome resistance to change and acknowledge their own influence on an analysis and that they are active observers. Friedman notes that despite these intellectual developments in psychoanalysis, there is a persistent utilization of the notion of objectivity and anonymity, which he believes conceals desires for omnipotence (see below) and privilege, which can harm the patient's well-being and personal development.

Friedman observes that although Merton Gill underscored the significance of Transference, he acknowledged that the patient's perception of the analyst has some basis in reality. Gill (1994a, p. 47) states that,

"My thesis is that the therapist should embrace the principle that whatever he does or does not do is an action that will have its interpersonal [and intrapsychic] meaning, that he has a major responsibility to search for this meaning, and, in interpreting that meaning, to recognize that his response (and here silence is a response) is a stimulus to bring about a response on the analysand's part. And the analysand's response will not simply be an irrational reaction without any basis in the ongoing interaction."

Gill, a prominent figure in modern analysis, highlights the influence of analyst actions, including silences, as possible triggers for the patient's transference reactions. He also furthered the idea of social constructivism within psychoanalysis. Although he stressed the analyst's role in shaping the therapeutic process, Gill (personal communication) affirmed the relevance of an objective reality. He warned against "anything goes" in some forms of contemporary psychoanalysis, expressing the worry that such an approach could be a "slippery slide into solipsism."

Similarly, Goldberg (1994) noted that the analyst is not an objective observer; instead, the analyst actively engages with the patient's inner world, seeking to unveil the meaning within the psychoanalytic context. The analyst is a participant who employs subjectivity, encompassing empathy and biases, in listening to patients.

After carefully studying the psychoanalytic process, many contemporary analysts have abandoned classical ideas of analytic objectivity, neutrality, abstinence, and anonymity. Many analysts focus on intersubjectivity, broadly exploring the co-created constructs emerging from the patient and analyst's mutually interacting selves (Stolorow et al., 1994; Stolorow, 1997). Ogden (2004), influenced by Winnicott's (1960) notion that there is no such thing as an infant apart from the mother, emphasized that clinical psychoanalysis is fundamentally an intersubjective process, relying on the relationship between the subjective reality of the analysand, the subjective reality of the analyst, and the intersubjective reality (the analytic third) created by the interaction of the former two.

Friedman suggests that the traditional model of the neutral, abstinent, and anonymous analyst carried an assumption of privilege. This positioning granted the psychoanalyst the belief that they inherently knew the true nature of what was happening with a patient, "no matter how much the patient found an interpretation to be wrong, irrelevant or harmful." According to Friedman, this attitude was fraught with the danger of the analyst assuming "omnipotence" in the analytic setting.

The God's-eye view proposed by Edelman, coupled with the

certainty accompanying such an assumption and the grandiosity suggested by Friedman, implies underlying unconscious inclinations inherent in the notions of objectivity. These concepts indicate a perspective transcending individual subjectivity, providing a comprehensive and assured vantage point. Edelman's idea of a God's-eye view implies omniscience and certainty, and Friedman's reference to grandiosity hints at an unconscious inflated sense of importance and privilege. These unconscious inclinations could involve a desire for certainty and a sense of superiority linked to the belief in an objective, all-encompassing viewpoint. Examining these psychological nuances becomes essential in understanding how deep-seated, unconscious motivations may influence the pursuit of objectivity in various disciplines.

The new definition of Transference

Gill advocated starting the therapeutic focus with actual experiences and interactions in the present moment. This approach diverged from a strictly one-person psychology (focusing primarily on the patient's intrapsychic dynamics) and moved towards a two-person psychology, highlighting the importance of the patient-therapist relationship.

Gill (1984) argued for a new definition of Transference, according to which both the analyst and patient inevitably contribute to the Transference. Gill's view, implicating both the patient and analyst in the production of Transference, contrasts with Freud's and a traditionally held view that the Transference was a product of the patient alone.

For example, Gill (1994a), following his new definition of Transference, developed a constructivist paradigm for psychoanalysis, and stated, "Analyst and analysand are in a continuous mutual interaction, each participating in shaping the other, and that not only is the knowledge of each about the psychic reality of the other being constructed in the immediate interaction but the assessment of previous interactions is likewise a construction. Neither participant can be unequivocal about the psychic reality of the other.

The understanding each has of the other is always partial, selective, and seen through his or her own psychic reality. The implications for technique of such a view are far reaching. They involve an essential recasting of every significant psychoanalytic dimension [p. 199].

Countertransference

In contrast to the earlier generation of analysts who believed in the effectiveness of the blank-screen approach for ensuring neutrality, analysts began to encounter surprises when clinical phenomena linked to the analyst's unconscious emerged. Analysts started acknowledging and exploring their episodic countertransference reactions to patients. For example, Lucia Tower (1956) forgot about a patient's session altogether, leading to a lapse in calendar scheduling, and she subsequently authored a groundbreaking paper on countertransference. Winnicott (1949) discussed experiencing hate in the countertransference. Analysts recognized the limits of relying on the blank screen. The analyst's unconscious and private life could unexpectedly make their presence felt in the analysis. The analyst's countertransference was no longer a private secret, but a phenomenon intertwined with the patient's Transference.

A traditional analysis views the patient's Transference and the analyst's countertransference, when present, as related but distinct phenomena attributable to the patient or the analyst, respectively. When countertransference (narrow) is evident in traditional analysis, it is episodic and indicates pathology in the analyst that impairs the analysis and necessitates some analyst's action. However, if the analyst detects no countertransference, he assumes he is objective, neutral, and reasonably error-free, providing the patient with accurate interpretations. Under such analytic conditions, where the analyst does not recognize his countertransference, exploring an analyst's bias is moot.

An analyst's assumption of objectivity and neutrality may be a dangerous illusion; without overt, undeniable evidence, analysts can continue to believe that their observations are unbiased. Such an assumption is often associated with the analyst's power and privilege. An unconscious collaboration between the analyst and patient may make it difficult for any analyst's bias to be detected and rectified. An analyst may consciously or unconsciously desire the privilege and powers of being a person of authority; simultaneously, it may also be the patient's conscious or unconscious wish to place the analyst in such an exalted position. The patient will likely be unaware of, or hesitate to, challenge a traditional psychoanalyst when this dynamic is present. Thus, there is an increased risk of patient compliance or agreement with the analyst. Because its detection relies on the analyst's self-awareness, in such circumstances, the risk in a traditional analysis is for the narrow countertransference to go undetected.

Contemporary analysts assume that analysts and patients mutually influence participants-observers. Thus, the patient's Transference and the analyst's countertransference are intertwined. Therefore, the analyst's broad countertransference is continuous, not episodic. This mutual influence on the countertransference can be summarized thus: Analysts experience specific memories, emotions, and anticipations evoked by their patient relationships and interactions; these responses, in turn, shape their assessments, interpretations, and actions. *When an analyst employs the notion of broad countertransference, the analysts must continuously account for influences and uncertainties introduced by the active participant-observer analysts throughout the analysis.* In contemporary treatments, the patient and analyst views help provide complementary perspectives. The patients' and analysts' perspectives may overlap or conflict in different areas. The patient and analyst, when feasible, collaboratively negotiate a shared understanding of a psychoanalytic event. Sometimes, they may agree to disagree, leaving the matter open for further resolution. The analyst cannot unilaterally decide its meaning.

Psychoanalytic principles and the assessment of Wild analysis[2]

Contradictions at times marked Freud's practical application of psychoanalysis as he sought to navigate a balance between rules he established for psychoanalytic technique and the foundational principles of analysis. While Freud articulated stringent rules governing psychoanalysis, he also presented numerous case examples grounded in psychoanalytic principles that, paradoxically, deviated from his own prescribed rules of technique. This tension reflects Freud's ongoing exploration and adaptation of his theoretical framework in response to the complexities of clinical reality. His followers faced a challenge: how to reconcile these two aspects of his legacy? If they focused on the rules, they would encounter a clash between technique and principles. They would honor his spirit of freedom if they accepted both or gave more weight to the principles and adjusted the rules of psychoanalytic technique to fit the case.

Freud (1913) described a rule of his practice, and then adjusted it as follows, "I work with my patients every day except on Sundays and public holidays—that is, as a rule, six days a week. For slight cases or the continuation of a treatment which is already well advanced, three days a week will be enough" p. 127. In the same paper, Freud cautioned against rigidly applying his rules, despite advocating for them, and wrote: "I think it is better to call these rules 'suggestions' and not demand any absolute adherence to them. The great variety of the psychic situations involved, the flexibility of all mental processes and the abundance of influencing factors resist any *mechanization of the technique* [italics mine]" p. 123.

Another aspect of the psychoanalytic technique involves the use of the couch. Freud (1912) revealed a personal motif for

[2]I thank Neal Spira, M.D., for his valuable suggestions concerning the section on Psychoanalytic principles and the assessment of Wild analysis.

choosing a couch as the tool for psychoanalytic treatment: he did not like being gazed at by others for long periods. Analysts often attempt to adhere to the rules of psychoanalytic technique, such as frequency, couch, neutrality, abstinence, and anonymity. Eissler (1953) noted that a parameter, a necessary departure from the standard psychoanalytic technique, is introduced when the basic model technique proves insufficient. General criteria for introducing a psychoanalytic parameter include (1) its use only when the standard model falls short; (2) ensuring it never exceeds the necessary minimum; (3) using it only if it eventually self-eliminates, concluding the treatment with a parameter set to zero. 4) Retrospective interpretations are the optimal tools for removing the effects of using a parameter. The dictates of psychoanalytic techniques and parameters have contributed to the practice of psychoanalysis.

Arnold Goldberg (1990) argues that the traditional foundations of psychoanalysis are so restrictive and restricting that they theoretically, institutionally, and educationally imprison psychoanalysis and the analyst. The frequency of sessions and the extended use of the couch became established prerequisites for psychoanalysis. Consequently, many analysts considered a treatment that effectively delved into unconscious and Transference processes but deviated from these technical norms as not genuinely reflective of psychoanalysis. Friedman's paper, addressing neutrality, abstinence, and anonymity, sheds light on another aspect of the pervasive and damaging results stemming from some psychoanalytic techniques.

The history of psychoanalysis reveals that the considerations of psychoanalytic technique determine deviations from the norm. The characterization of a "wild analysis" has often revolved around discussions of technique and parameters. At times, deeming an analysis as wild has involved dismissing a treatment due to its incorporation of interpersonal considerations rather than focusing solely on intrapsychic factors or including elements of psychotherapy.

What measures have analysts taken to address the prevalent overreliance on psychoanalytic techniques and their mechanization, which appears to have constrained them?

In keeping with the need for flexibility in psychoanalytic techniques, Freud was not always consistent with his rules for psychoanalysis. Freud displayed a sparkling freedom from his rules of psychoanalytic rules. For instance, Freud (1909) recounted the analysis of Little Hans, wherein the boy's father communicated with Freud and conducted the analysis. Despite meeting Little Hans only once, Freud labeled his efforts as an "analysis."

Freud's "Wild analysis" discussion may point to another principled direction: a proper appreciation of psychoanalytic principles over preoccupation with psychoanalytic technique. Freud (1910) recounted the case of a divorced woman who had sought his opinion after being dissatisfied with the vulgar counsel of her regular physician, who had claimed to be applying psychoanalytic principles. The physician had suggested that the woman's anxiety would only be alleviated by either reconciling with her ex-husband, engaging in an affair, or resorting to masturbation.

The woman opposed the doctor's suggested cure because it required her to enter into a liaison or to masturbate, both of which were repugnant to her on moral and religious grounds. She was unwilling to return to her former husband.

Freud maintained that analytic interventions are wild unless the analyst meets two preconditions: Firstly, the analyst must have already conducted a sufficient preparatory analysis of resistance to bring the repressed material very close to consciousness. Secondly, the analysand must have already formed a transference attachment to the analyst, ensuring they do not flee from the analysis as the repressed material emerges.

In this example, Freud exposes the poor and erroneous use of psychoanalytic concepts by the woman's regular doctor.

The doctor's recommendations are superficial and inadequate, failing to capture the complexity and richness of proper psychoanalytic practice. They also show a distorted and misinformed application of Freudian principles. This anecdote illustrates the kind of "wild psychoanalysis" that Freud denounced—cases where individuals, without a solid grasp of psychoanalytic theory, provide simplistic and potentially harmful interpretations and advice to those seeking psychological help. Furthermore, this illustration underscores Freud's recognition of the significance of the patient's perspective and its role in assigning value to a treatment. The analyst must include the patient's perspective in his assessment.

Freud's concepts regarding the criteria for determining "wildness" appear most relevant for guiding analytic thinking according to the principles of analysis rather than technical elements that may vary from one case to another. Freud's definition of "wildness" is not contingent on factors like the frequency of sessions, the use of the couch, neutrality, abstinence, or anonymity. Instead, it is grounded in considerations of unconscious processes, transference dynamics, and resistance factors.

Freud (1914, p. 16), stressing the principles of psychoanalysis, stated:

"It may thus be said that the theory of psychoanalysis is an attempt to account for two striking and unexpected facts of observation which emerge whenever an attempt is made to trace the symptoms of a neurotic back to their sources in his past life: the facts of Transference and resistance. Any line of investigation which recognizes these two facts and takes them as the starting point of its work may call itself psychoanalysis though it arrives at results other than my own."

To emphasize the lasting value of these principles and the role of unconscious processes in guiding psychoanalysis rather than fixed rules of technique, I (Sripada, 2015) defined

Essential Psychoanalysis as any line of treatment, theory, or science that recognizes unconscious, Transference, or resistance and takes them as the starting point of its work, regardless of its results.

This definition of psychoanalysis is limited to clinical analysis, which aims to understand and assist the patient. It does not address training analysis, which balances the candidate analysts' educational goals and the patient's clinical demands (either of the candidate as a patient or the candidate's patient).

Contemporary analysis considering two-person psychology and the participant observer.

There are many ways to conceptualize contemporary psychoanalysis; this is my version's summary. As participant-observers with different histories, perspectives, and interests, the patient and analyst co-create and contribute to the analysis's Unconscious, Transference, and Resistance processes. Analysts' actions frustrate or gratify patients to varying degrees. The analyst is aware that he authentically reveals himself through his presence and in every aspect of his attitudes and interactions. To alleviate patient suffering and enhance the patient's well-being and freedom, the analyst employs interpretations, containment, empathy, and judgment and learns from the analyst's prediction errors and feedback in the analytic relationship.

Unconscious, Transference, and Resistance are not categorical terms but represent the following dimensions: unconscious-preconscious-conscious, transference-countertransference, and resistance and facilitatory factors.

Practitioners from various schools of Psychoanalysis acknowledge the dimensions associated with the Unconscious, Transference, and Resistance processes. Therefore, there are instinctual, structural, Oedipal, metapsychological, relational, self-psychological, intersubjective, developmental, hermeneutic, and neuropsychoanalytic variants of

Unconscious, Transference, and Resistance in contemporary psychoanalysis.

A contemporary analyst does not claim any advantage or authority from being "objective," "neutral," "impartial," or seen as "the exalted ideal analyst." The contemporary analyst's strength lies in providing interpretations and perspectives, which can help the patient gain insight, make better choices, and foresee outcomes that can reduce distress and symptoms, enhance relationships with others in the patient's life, and increase self-awareness.

A contemporary analyst refrains from presenting interpretations as conclusive or definitive statements regarding the patient's situation. Instead, these interpretations are provisional opinions—tentative perspectives that the patient is encouraged to explore, test, and assess for their practical value.

The active participant observer and intersubjectivity are core principles that guide the contemporary psychoanalyst's work. They allow him to exercise his freedom, autonomy, and discernment based on these values, regardless of the outcomes. (The analyst's demonstration of freedom in thought, imagination, emotion, and action within the present therapeutic relationship can serve as a live experience for the patient. This demonstration may incidentally offer models for patient identifications, potentially fostering an expansion of the patient's own freedoms.)

The analyst remains dedicated to the core principles of psychoanalysis, with the overarching goal of alleviating the patient's suffering and enhancing their well-being. The analyst understands that each therapeutic journey is unique and requires flexibility and adaptability. Therefore, they do not strictly follow traditional psychoanalytic norms but rather adjust them to the needs of each case. Instead, the analyst tailors the psychoanalytic approach to each patient's unique dynamics and needs, considering their current challenges.

Analysts can access their external and internal perceptions, thoughts, imaginations, emotions, possible actions, and evoked memories. An analyst using broad countertransference uses the analyst's own experiences for analytic understanding and to interpret the patient's inner world. The analyst's experiences might relate to the patient's experiences, thoughts, feelings, fantasies, actions, conflicts, stresses, self-image, and relationships. This broad countertransference is like a living laboratory that gives clues to the analyst about some possible insight, empathy, interpretation, or action the pursuing of which may be beneficial to the patient. The analysts should freely use any such countertransference guidance to initiate preliminary actions. The analyst's action starts the negotiation process with the patient, which may result in a shared view. It may also result in rejection, or the idea may require further time for additional assessments. The analyst, ideally, should welcome the patient's rejection of an interpretation, for it signifies the opportunity for further evaluation and a reflection of the patient's freedom to disagree with the analyst. However, a contemporary analyst may also experience countertransference that is so intense or prolonged that it interferes with or disrupts the patient's analysis. When countertransference interferes with the treatment, it becomes necessary for the analyst to seek consultation, enter a personal analysis, or transfer the case to another analyst.

I (Sripada, 2022) recently published a memoir to clarify the two-person active participant observer concept and provide a clinical demonstration of the interconnected transference and countertransference phenomena. This narrative explores the treatment of a severely depressed patient, offering a comprehensive account from the perspective of a first-person analyst. The memoir illustrates the advantages, both for the patient and the analyst, of embracing a more liberated approach that departs from traditional rules of psychoanalytic technique while still adhering to the foundational principles of psychoanalysis, including the detailed clinical exploration of the unconscious, understanding transference, and addressing resistance.

Conclusion

The foundation of all psychoanalysis lies in the patient's free associations, the analyst's interpretations and actions, and the psychoanalytic principles of the Unconscious, Transference, and Resistance. Traditional psychoanalytic techniques rely heavily on an objective, neutral, abstinent, and anonymous analyst. In contrast, contemporary psychoanalysis embraces a participant-observer approach within a two-person psychology. Here, the analyst's manifest reality or unconscious or conscious active-participant-observations contribute to the analytic situation and the patient's transference. The analyst recognizes that their presence and actions can evoke varying degrees of frustration or gratification in the patient. This contemporary perspective acknowledges that analysts reveal themselves through their very being and all actions in the analytic situation. A broad countertransference encompasses the analyst's perceptions, thoughts, imaginations, emotions, actions, and evoked memories. The broad countertransference serves as a dual indicator of the analyst's personality and a laboratory reflection of the patient's conflicts, stresses, Self, and other identifications.

The divergence between traditional and contemporary psychoanalysis rests on significant technical assumptions. Despite theoretical departures from traditional instinct-based Oedipal theory and ego psychology, Friedman argues that many contemporary analysts still adhere to psychoanalytic technical norms such as neutrality, abstinence, and anonymity. He notes a lack of a sufficiently robust active analyst technique within the framework of two-person psychology.

This paper, along with Friedman's, explores factors contributing to analysts' hesitation, including unconscious or conscious attachment to the idea of the analyst's objectivity, a preference for the certainty of a God's-eye perspective, a desire for idealization, issues of privilege, power, and grandiosity, fear of solipsism, and concerns about criticism or being labeled as a "wild" analyst or as practicing psychotherapy rather than analysis.

Those championing contemporary psychoanalysis and seeking transformative change are responsible for developing, articulating, and advocating for a new psychoanalytic technique—one that embraces the analyst's active participation as an observer within a two-person intersubjective framework. I strongly encourage all contemporary analysts who believe in both the analyst and patient as active participant observers to share comprehensive reports of their treatments.

These reports should delve into significant details highlighting the co-creative nature of the analytic space and events within the two-person dynamic. Additionally, analysts should provide in-depth descriptions of their broad countertransference experiences, which serve as a crucial laboratory for understanding tentative patient dynamics. Furthermore, patient-analyst differences and the analyst's prediction errors, whether identified through the analyst's self-diagnosis or pointed out by the patient, represent crucial starting points for negotiations and learning from analytic errors. These errors warrant significant attention and should be prominent in analytic descriptions. Analysts are encouraged to articulate their active involvement in the analytic process, their contributions to the patient's experiences of frustration and gratification, and instances of self-revelation. A vital part of analytic communications is addressing such contributions throughout the treatment.

Whenever possible, analysts should transparently communicate the source of their countertransference so their peers can better understand their interpretations and interventions. Such detailed descriptions of collaborative patient-analyst interactions and negotiations will benefit future patients, contribute to the advancement of psychoanalysis, and provide valuable insights for a broader understanding of humanity.

References

Arlow, J.A., & Brenner, C. (1964). *Psychoanalytic Concepts and the Structural Theory.* Madison, CT: International Universities Press.

Brenner, C. (1994). The Mind as Conflict and Compromise Formation. *Journal of Clinical Psychoanalysis* 3:473–488.

Comte, Auguste (1855). *Positive Philosophy of Auguste Comte, Part I,* H. Martineau (transl). Whitefish, MT: Kessinger Publishing, 2003.

Descartes, R. (1968). Meditation IV, *In The Philosophical Works of Descartes,* E.S. Haldane, C.H., L.L.D. and G.R.T. Ross, M.A., D.Phil. (transl). Volume I, Cambridge: Cambridge University Press, 1968.

Downing, Lisa, "George Berkeley," *The Stanford Encyclopedia of Philosophy* (Fall 2021 Edition), Edward N. Zalta (ed.), URL: https://plato.stanford.edu/archives/fall2021/entries/berkeley/.

Edelman, G.M. (1992). *Bright Air, Brilliant Fire: On the Matter of the Mind.* New York: Basic Books.

Eissler, K.R. (1953). The Effect of the Structure of the Ego on Psychoanalytic Technique. *Journal of the American Psychoanalytic* Association 1:104–143.

Freud, S. (1893). The Psychotherapy of Hysteria from *Studies on Hysteria. Standard Edition* 2:253–305, p. 282.

——— (1910). 'Wild' Psycho-Analysis. *Standard Edition* 11:219–228.

————— (1914b). On the history of the psycho-analytic movement. *Standard Edition* 14:1–66.

————— (1933). New Introductory Lectures On Psycho-Analysis. *Standard Edition* 22:1–182, pp. 170–171.

————— (1909). Analysis of a phobia in a five-year-old boy. *Standard Edition* 10:1–150.

————— (1912). Recommendations to Physicians Practicing Psycho-analysis. *Standard Edition* 12:109–120.

Friedman, H.J. (2020). The Need for and Resistance to Realness in the Analyst: Making Psychoanalysis a Truly Two-Person Experience. *Psychoanalytic Inquiry* 40:262–270.

Gabbard, G.O. & Ogden, T.H. (2009). On Becoming a Psychoanalyst. *International Journal of Psychoanalysis* 90:311–327.

Galatzer-Levy, R.M. (1991). Introduction: *Self Psychology Searches for Its Self. Progress in Self-Psychology* 7:xi–xviii.

Gill, M.M. (1984). Transference: A Change in Conception or Only in Emphasis? *Psychoanalytic Inquiry* 4:489–523.

————— (1994a). *Psychoanalysis in Transition: A Personal View.* Hillsdale, NJ: The Analytic Press.

————— (1994b). Heinz Kohut's self-psychology. *A Decade of Progress: Progress in Self Psychology, Vol. 10,* ed. A. Goldberg. Hillsdale, NJ: The Analytic Press, pp. 197–211.

Goldberg, A. (1990). *The Prisonhouse of Psychoanalysis.* Hillsdale, NJ: The Analytic Press.

————— (1994). Farewell to the objective analyst. *International Journal of Psycho-Analysis* 75:21–30.

Grimes, J. (2004). *The Vivekacudamani of Sankaracarya Bhagavatpada: An Introduction and Translation.* New Delhi: Motilal Banarsidass Publishers, p. 222–223.

Heisenberg, W. (1958). *Physics and Philosophy: The Revolution in Modern Science.* New York: Harper & Row, p. 50.

Kant, I. (1781). *Critique of Pure Reason,* N.K. Smith, (ed). New York: Macmillan, 1929.

Ogden, T. (2004). The analytic third: Implications for psychoanalytic theory and technique *Psychoanalytic Quarterly* 73:167–95.

Raju. P.T. (1953). *Idealistic Thought Of India.* London: George Allen and Unwin Ltd, p. 116.

Schwaber, E.A. (2005). The Struggle to Listen: Continuing Reflections, Lingering Paradoxes, and Some Thoughts on Recovery of Memory. *Journal of the American Psychoanalytic Association* 53:789–810.

Skibba, R. (2018). Einstein, Bohr, and the war over quantum theory. *Nature* 559–560, p. 555.

Sripada, B. (2015). Essential Psychoanalysis: Toward a Re-Appraisal of the Relationship between Psychoanalysis and Dynamic Psychotherapy. *Psychodynamic Psychiatry* 43(3):396–422. doi: 10.1521/pdps.2015.43.3.396.

——— (2022). *When Suicide Beckons: A Psychoanalyst's Memoir.* Chicago: Essential Psychoanalysis Press.

Stolorow, R. (1997). Dynamic, dyadic, intersubjective systems: An evolving paradigm for psychoanalysis. *Psychoanalytic Psychology* 14:337–346.

Stolorow, R.D. Atwood, G.E. Brandchaft, B. (1994). *The intersubjective perspective.* Northvale, NJ: Aronson.

Winnicott, D.W. (1960). Ego distortion in terms of true and false self. In *The Maturational Processes and the Facilitating Environment.* New York: International Universities Press, 1965.

Chapter 3
Comments on "The Problem with Psychoanalytic Anonymity: The Obstacles Created by the Persistence of Traditional Technique"

Lance Dodes

This paper underscores important technical problems that have historically been present in psychoanalysis, and suggests a major technical shift to address them. The proposed new paradigm is summarized as a "give and take" between analyst and patient, a conversation in which the analyst shares personal information (self-discloses) in order to helpfully use the "real" relationship in the room.

The author acknowledges that many current analysts believe the traditional technique he describes has mostly died out. To the degree that practice has now modified technique to be free of the major "traditional" problems, the need for a major further change is less. All improvement is important, however, with the caveat that it does not either discard what remains useful from the past or introduce new problems. This issue is the focus of my commentary.

The "traditional" analyst

The "traditional" analyst is described as someone who has "remained under the influence of Freud's theoretical and technical vision of what constituted psychoanalysis" and in practice is "very silent ... seldom heard ... the purveyor of analytic proof. ... [B]y remaining anonymous [he] gains from a mysteriousness that implies an all knowing or magical persona ... His feelings were to be seen as countertransference and, as such, needed to be contained, split off, for his own consideration but not to be shared with the patient." For this analyst, the "search for the intra-psychic conflicts was the exclusive arena for psychoanalysis [versus a view that] the nature of the environment that a patient developed in greatly influenced the problems in living that each patient experienced in adult life."

This is a reasonable description; many of us in the field grew up with it.

Is this a picture of today's psychoanalyst?

Although they may exist, I'd expect that few living analysts fail to recognize the role of the environment in shaping their patients. There probably are still analysts who appear to their patients to be mysterious, perhaps because they speak little. But with today's mainstream awareness of two-person psychology and decades of thinking, or at least hearing about, relational technique, I don't believe there are many who believe that being mysterious is a good idea, or would wish to appear magical as an aid for treatment. Similarly, the traditional analyst is described as seeing every communication from a patient as transference and failing to see his or her role as a real person. I believe most of our colleagues today would view that as simply bad practice.

Of course, in any field there will be people who are behind the times. We do need to remain alert to the problems of old and rigid technique where they still occur.

The proposed new technique

Key to this paper is the view that historical progress in understanding patients was not accompanied by a corresponding change in technique. It proposes a specific alteration in technique: "real give and take or conversation between two adults," principally through greater self-disclosure by the analyst. The paper asserts that the reason this technique is not used is that: "If the details of the analyst's background or his political views or religious observation...have been disclosed, or enter into the analytic dialogue, it has been assumed that this will truncate the development of the supposedly necessary 'transference neurosis' ".

In recent times, emphasis on the concept of a transference neurosis has declined as it has been recognized to be absent or only partially present in many successful analyses. Interfering with it is therefore probably less an objection to self-disclosure than in the past. Self-disclosure remains a source of significant concern for other reasons, however, as I will discuss later.

The paper also states, "the interdiction against self-disclosure [should be] dropped along with the insistence on neutrality and abstinence." Neutrality ideally refers to remaining "neutral to the patient's conflict" (Hoffer) in order to make the treatment situation safe for the patient to express his thoughts and feelings without fear of the analyst's disapproval, and to allow their free investigation. Abstinence refers to refraining from enactments which arise from unconsidered emotional response to a patient's affects or actions. There is nothing inherently problematic with these ideas. Specifically, neutrality and abstinence do not prevent discussion of an analyst's personal views if that is deemed useful at a particular moment in the treatment. Accepting a place for self-disclosure does not provide any reason to drop neutrality and abstinence as defined above.

The paper also emphasizes the need to lessen focus on transference and countertransference because of concern that this interferes with attending to the reality of the analyst and patient and their interaction as "real" people. Again, good current treatment attends to both transference and countertransference as well as the "real" relationship in the room. The balance between focus on transference/countertransference and the "real" relationship will depend on what must be attended to at any point in treatment, and will necessarily be different with different patients. It would mean abandonment of a great deal of the nature of psychoanalysis to, in general, lessen focus on transference and countertransference to a secondary level.

A similar view applies to self-disclosure. It may be important, or even essential, with some patients at some times. But it is widely understood that there are just as clearly times and patients where it would be destructive.

Consider a patient who suspects that he knows the analyst's view on a topic (religion, etc.) and to whom it is important to know that his perceptions/guesses are valid and respected, or that his analyst is going to be honest with him, since his parents were not. The analyst needs to appreciate whatever is the meaning to his patient at that point. It may indeed be essential that he answer the patient's questions to show the respect, validation and honesty the patient needs to see at this moment. To be clear, the analyst is not here being false or "unreal". He does respect the patient and is honest with him. He is simply being thoughtful in his intentional choice of response. And, in this circumstance, if the analyst tells the patient his religion or his favored political party, neither neutrality nor abstinence is breached by this response.

But consider another example. An analyst reveals his memories of playing baseball with his father as a child. This may carry the meaning to his patient of being understood, included, valued and perhaps loved. It can be actively helpful in learning from a "new" relationship. But we can easily imagine a patient being damaged by the analyst revealing his personal history or views, because they repeat a relationship with an intrusive self-preoccupied parent whose narcissistic focus left the patient alone, depressed and enraged. Or, the analyst's self-disclosure may have a problematic meaning to the patient about the analyst which becomes a hard truth for the patient since it is seen as fact, because it was not the patient's fantasy but was revealed by the analyst. This meaning may create a lasting block that is very difficult to discover. There are of course other possible problems with telling a patient factual details of the analyst's life, including unspoken envy, disgust, anger, or an assumption of shared meaning ("You're from my country, I can now assume without discussion that we share views of this issue").

With some patients at some points in treatment, intentional self-disclosure by an analyst might lead to the kind of "give and take" to which the paper refers. And for some patients an overall "give and take" relationship may be exactly what the patient needs. But this cannot be an overall recommendation for psychoanalytic technique because it does not apply to all patients most of the time or some patients any of the time.

Harm from "traditional" technique

The paper makes its strongest point in favor of greater self-disclosure and give-and-take in the observation that, "when talking to individuals who have had a traditional psychoanalysis...what they recall about what was important to them in their experience of their analyst was some small moment of unexpected human exchange with the analyst." I very much agree that "traditional" technique often failed badly to recognize the impact and meaning to a patient of the analyst's withdrawn or aloof demeanor. It caused a great deal of harm by reproducing traumatic abandonment and loneliness, and worsening already existing self-doubt.

In my view, the major protection against such retraumatization is to be aware of its risk. All therapists must look for and understand their patients' (usually deep) need to be heard, valued and feel cared for. Therapists must be aware that there will be times that self-disclosure is essential, and be the most helpful way to address these fundamental issues.

Conclusion

This paper reminds us of the dangers of an aloof, rigid, mysterious analyst, as seen in "traditional" technique. Keeping these warnings in mind, most of us are doing better. Modern psychoanalytic technique includes awareness that there are two idiosyncratic people in the room, neither of whom is omniscient. Most of us today agree with a central theme of this paper that self-disclosure should not be seen as a technical error or forbidden, but rather as a valuable option for the therapist. However, I do not agree with the paper that self-disclosure resulting in a "give-and-take" conversation should be the aim of psychoanalytic technique. Self-disclosure ought to be introduced with the same thoughtfulness as any other action or speech of the therapist, bearing in mind its potential problems. Its introduction depends entirely on what will be helpful and usable to the patient at the time.

We must avoid being the unavailable, retraumatizing, distant analyst of the past. We must attend to our patients' need for recognition, validation and respect, which may require self-disclosure at particular moments. That does not have to come at the expense of our awareness and focus on transference, countertransference, intrapsychic conflict, neutrality and abstinence.

Reference

Hoffer, Axel (1985). Toward a Definition of Psychoanalytic Neutrality. *JAPA* 33:771–795.

Chapter 4
BOTH: The Imperative of Dialectical Process

Deana Schuplin

I am honored to be asked to contribute this response to Henry Friedman essay titled "The Problem with Psychoanalytic Anonymity: The Obstacles Created by the Persistence of Traditional Technique" for a journal whose mission is laudable. The invitation comes because of my piping in, something I do occasionally, on APsA's list serve in response to Henry's post titled "Dividing Psychoanalysts into Categories" where he advocated for his point in this essay. I do that because I am a debater. I have been a debater since grade school. Not in any formal sense but as a means of relating to my father. I'm going to disclose some about that to frame my response, and as I was drafting this, I realized it may be able to make a point for Henry's case, or maybe not. We'll see.

In the first educational session I had as a psychoanalytic candidate we were introducing ourselves. I ended up being last, and I thought as I listened to everyone talk about their history and how they got there, I was out of place. I didn't, and don't, doubt that I can learn about and practice psychoanalysis.

What I did feel is that I am different. I said to my fellow candidate, that there is nothing in my background, no previous analysis, no parents who were analyst, no academic exposure to Freud's ideas, save a lone class with a lone concept from somebody who followed Freud, which would indicate I would end up here.

At that point I had primarily been a substance use disorder therapist who had worked for too long with difficult cases. I was intentionally referred these cases and was dedicated to the work, but I was alone in it. My colleagues at the time were not as curious or invested in this kind of work. CBT, Family Systems, Client Centered, DBT and Gestalt methods were insufficient to the task at hand as I experienced them. When I found a community of psychoanalysts, I felt like I found somewhere that I could now share the process of trying to understand the inexplicable and intractable aspects of our patient's struggles and find out a way to help them.

As I have been deeply and gratefully involved in psychoanalytic practice and education over the years since, I have found something else. It is what seems to me to be the fallout of conflict that began with Freud and his colleagues but never got or gets worked through. It is like an active and open wound that gets played out over and over again, without seeming to heal or move forward. I have felt its sway many times, sometimes from a distance, and sometimes quite close. It seems to me that it has caused splits in our community and confusing branches of our theory that use different language to talk about the same thing and fight with or even dismiss one another when my impression is that they do not disagree as much as their arguments would indicate. As a case in point, I want to return to discussions on APsaA's list serv. I have often, when I can keep up with it, found many discussions there proceed with many of the same people, making the same points with more and more words that then escalate into hostility. This is followed by objections to the hostility and then objections to the objections. I want to take up the question of how we might better be able to move the discussions forward, evolve rather than devolve. I have no trouble with disagreement that is passionate, vehement and even hostile. It is the repetitiveness that gets my attention, particularly when I consider the impact of past wounds within the psychoanalytic community that I have encountered. Is the source of our being stuck with unresolved conflicts, unresolved trauma?

I'm going to try to say something about this in my response and offer, for your consideration, what I've learned from having engaged throughout my life in open and contentious debate with people I love. As a result of arguing for decades, I have come to different points of synthesis. I hope that by approaching this controversial debate from the novel angle of my personal experience, I can contribute something to the discussion moving forward.

I'll turn to some more self-disclosure. In the past decade, my husband and I have been members of The Prairie Club, a monthly member only dinner club where those members rotate presenting research papers that are out of their area of expertise. After the paper is read there is a significant period of discussion. In the early days of this 125-year-old club, which used to be exclusively, white men with rank and/or power, the debates would often become quite hostile and raucous. A cartoon depicting the club around that time showed members punching, choking, knifing and swinging chairs at each other, while several others hid under the table. This tradition evolved when they began giving cryptic titles to prevent members doing research on the subject to aid them in mounting attack during the discussion. As a result, there was not an option to come to the discussion loaded for bear. It is my observation that many individuals within our community are hiding or loaded for bear. I think I observe this in Henry.

The first paper that I presented to the club was entitled BOTH (my version of a cryptic name where the topic was how to evolve our long-standing debate around capitalism versus socialism). Writing this paper gave me a chance to research areas related to the debate I've been having with my father from my early days in college until around a decade ago when our focus turned to dealing with aging and, as a retired engineer, his exploration of physics. I am going to excerpt heavily from that paper to lay out my experience and views. This title parallels my response to Henry on the list serve where I piped that I could not imagine working as a psychoanalyst without having the resources of engagement from a stance of some amount of anonymity **and** work in the real relationship.

Dialectical thinking is central to the awareness that I gained writing this paper. The discussions/debates I have had over the years, my own thinking about the nature of the associated conflicts and what I discovered as I researched this paper made me more and more appreciative of the value of ever evolving, dialectical dialogue. This developmental process involves a thesis that gives rise to its reaction, an antithesis, which contradicts or negates the thesis. Then the tension between the two is resolved by means of a synthesis. In APsA there seems to be plenty of tension. The question, as I see it, is how to proceed to more synthesis. How do we give due consideration to both the thesis and the antithesis? I see this as a necessary part of moving forward toward synthesis. Here is something of how I got there.

My father and I began debating long before I went to college. We drove my mother and my little sister crazy. But that was only part of the fun. In grade school it was whether our Mercury Comet was green or blue. The name of the color is Chrysler Turquoise. In high school it was whether you go through or over a mountain pass. I don't have any reference for that, and I don't remember whether I advocated for green and over or blue and through, but I remember being passionate about it. When I decided to study social work in college, my father was concerned. He had been liberal in his thinking when I was younger but became an evangelical Christian during my high school years and his views had grown more conservative. He thought I would be swayed by secular humanism. He was right and our debates turned to more serious topics. Whoever was present in the household had to endure our raised voices over longer and longer periods of time. But because we knew and loved each other, our arguing was a form of play, and therefore this did not alienate me from my father but actually drew us closer.

This does not mean that I wasn't convinced of the absolute rightness of my case. Over time I found myself wondering why my dad's line of reasoning even existed. How could people think this way? But since this was my father, I was never loaded for bear. As I was vigorously advocating for my position, it was often reinforced in my coursework. On the one hand, I was becoming more and more convinced. At the same time, I was also ingesting other kinds of input. My senior year of college, I read through the whole Bible. I had a fair amount of time on my hands and achieving this goal took up some of it. I think it was in the context of arguing with my father the relative merits of a socialist versus a capitalist system that this verse stood out to me:

Leviticus 25:8–13 "And thou shalt number seven sabbaths of years unto thee, seven times seven years; and the space of the seven sabbaths of years shall be unto thee forty and nine years. Then shalt thou cause the trumpet of the jubilee to sound on the tenth day of the seventh month, in the day of atonement shall ye make the trumpet sound throughout all your land. And ye shall hallow the fiftieth year, and proclaim liberty throughout all the land unto all the inhabitants thereof: it shall be a jubilee unto you; and ye shall return every man unto his possession, and ye shall return every man unto his family. A jubilee shall that fiftieth year be unto you: ye shall not sow, neither reap that which groweth of itself in it, nor gather the grapes in it of thy vine undressed. For it is the jubile; it shall be holy unto you: ye shall eat the increase thereof out of the field. In the year of this jubile ye shall return every man unto his possession."

I immediately interpreted this as a mix of the two; a period of capitalism interspersed with an act of socialism. Wouldn't this be a way to have the best of both? Over the years I have asked many people if they were familiar with the year of jubilee and many were, but their understanding didn't include competition interspersed with redistribution. Why? Do we inherently have difficulty with the idea of integrating the two? Do we end up in our respective corners fighting for our chosen side without the capacity to consider the merits of the other's perspective?

Based on my limited research within Judaism, jubilee was never fully, and certainly not repeatedly, enacted over time. The corruption of this idea was furthered by its application within Catholicism where it was most consistently used to increase inequality with very few exceptions. Here, a seeming synthesis is offered at the outset. But I suppose it cannot be a synthesis since the process of the development of the thesis, then the antithesis, with the resulting conflict where they have it out, before integrating something from each into the synthesis.

The lack of synthesis of the ideas of capitalism and socialism can be seen in the United States in terms of ongoing conflict and division. The disruption remains even though we, like the vast majority of countries in the world, have a synthesis of the two in the form of mixed-market economies. This conflict, along with being disruptive in and of itself, limits our capacity to more meaningfully consider the relative merits and downsides which would allow us to improve our application of both.

Another reference point with an eye to conflict in my process of writing my Prairie Club paper is the only first line of a novel that ever got stuck in my mind. "It was the best of times; it was the worst of times." This, I'm sure many of you recognize, is from *A Tale of Two Cities*. It, of course, refers to the two cities, London and Paris. At the outset circumstances were better in London than in Paris, of course depending on who you were. But Paris saw more revolutionary change of a kind that some idealize today. Liberty, Equality, Fraternity.

What's not to like?

But Dickens was willing to include the ugliness that went along with rapid change to a horrific governing system. The ugliness can be summed up as "off with all their heads". Though it took a long time for things to stabilize, we benefit from these changes to this day and I'm sure will well into the future. But does resistance to further change in the form of additional revolution stem from the violence that accompanied this transformation? I understood the first line as declaring that in the course of positive change there is the potential for bad outcomes too; the unintended consequence that we ignore at our peril.

On the other hand, London was stable, a good thing, but good change was less possible, even though inequality was rampant there too.

We all want positive change, but I think it is a tricky thing. A famous quote from Will and Ariel Durant, Pulitzer Prize winners for general nonfiction and authors of *The Story of Civilization,* describe an aspect of this. "Nothing is clearer in history than the adoption by successful rebels of the methods they were accustomed to condemn in the forces they deposed."

Of course, we know that the world is not black or white. Knowing that and living it are two different things. I think we tend to feel our approaches are right and other's approaches are wrong. It's difficult to maintain an open mind about more than one way to solve a problem and keep in mind that in each solution there are downsides. So, we cannot easily arrive at an option that includes both.

One way to cultivate the capacity to embrace both, giving us a chance to create a synthesis, is curiosity about the rest of the story. What is there that I don't know about the current situation or person I am dealing with? What is the rest of the story that is going to play out after this current event? What good might come from the application of the other's approach? What bad might come when things are solved my way?

The point I am trying to make is akin to one made by Grace Lee Boggs, someone I discovered while I was researching my paper, BOTH. I want to share what I learned from her thoughts about how to resolve impasses on a whole other level of magnitude.

She both turned 100 and passed away in 2015. Here is some of her history.

Grace was active in the communist and black rights movements since her days facing down rats to get to the basement of a Jewish woman's home where she lived for free in Chicago when she couldn't get professional work as a Chinese American woman. She was inspired by A. Philip Randolph's 1941 threat to march on Washington that gave him leverage to extract from FDR an executive order to ban discrimination against African Americans in war era jobs. Hopeful about the potential to bring about change in the face of injustice, she espoused Malcolm X's brand of activism until she questioned the violence that erupted in the 60's civil rights movement when after 5 days, 43 people were dead. At this point she more fully considered Martin Luther King Junior's ideas of non-violence and ended up adding them to Malcolm's militancy.

As she observed the lack of sustained improvement and real change despite progress in the civil rights movement along with the impact of globalization, industrialization and urbanization, Grace lamented that now workers ended up with no sense of themselves as a part of a community as had been the case when unions were initially formed. As she saw it, they felt like victims. She developed her conviction that an activist "must not be just against something but must be for something." This evolved in her thinking over time. In the 50's and 60's she worked for and watched revolutionary fights here and in Africa. As she saw the arc of events, she became aware of the illusion that uprising, rebellion and defiance were the solution since with them power structures could be collapsed. She began to realize that as yet there was little sense that something new had to be built. She was able to come to this realization in Detroit. She could see the shortcomings of rebellion that was "an explosion out of righteous grievance." While rebellion involves an outburst of anger and resistance, it is not revolution.

Grace Lee Boggs' experience with revolution's potential and shortcomings enriched her thinking. She had always studied ideas but began to emphasize them as an integral part of successful change. She espoused that "when you take a position you should try and examine what the implications are." As I have framed it, "what is the rest of the story?" Another way that she says this is "radical movements have overemphasized the role of activism and underemployed the role of reflection." So, as she elaborates this, the issue is not just the "oppressed versus the oppressor, but we have to change ourselves to change the world."

Grace pushes everyone to evolve their ideas, advocating that most people think ideas are fixed when ideas have power because they are not fixed. Once they become fixed they are already dead. James, her husband, and she writes in their book *Revolution and Evolution in The Twentieth Century* written in 1974, "(t)he most dangerous enemy of the revolutionary theoretician is not the external enemy but the potential within all theory, and especially the boldest theories, to become dogma. The more a revolutionary thinker is isolated from systematic dialogue and practical interaction with revolutionary social forces, the greater this danger."

Dialectical process is what I think Grace is describing when she talks about evolution. Evolution is by its nature is slow and unpredictable/uncontrollable since it is rooted in this dialectical, essentially developmental process. I think for synthesis to occur both parties need to remain engaged and to some degree open to one another. In the process of the evolution of The Prairie Club, they cultivated openness by preventing the collection of ammunition. A difficulty that we have is we've had the chance to load for bear over years and even decades.

This is my second to the last personal story. When I was new to Iowa, I was not used to all the large trucks in parking lots. They really don't fit. They take up more than one space most of the time, often because they aren't even parked straight. This bugged me. One day driving down the road near our home with my husband, I noticed a pickup truck parked about 3 feet from the curve. With the width of the street this meant that only one car could pass at a time. I began griping the first time we passed. When we returned, I was looking ahead to see if it was still there in the same spot. It was and my ire was escalating again. Then, as we got closer, I noticed an older gentleman sitting in the driver's seat. He didn't look like he was going anywhere; he was just sitting there. This new information changed my disposition toward the truck and, of course, the driver. There was a human face and one I couldn't as easily get mad at. But it still didn't make sense to me. Luckily, we had to go out again not long after returning home (my husband refuses to make a list for trips to the home improvement store—but that's another story). I was now more curious than worked up. As we approached the truck it was easy to see from a distance "the rest of the story". There was a tow truck. With this information I could imagine that the driver might not have been able to work the truck into a "proper" parking position before it died.

This simple story, along with the other material that I have elaborated, are meant to make a more complex point. Henry Friedman is advocating for change in the technique involving anonymity versus self-disclosure. This is an important question with the answer being better served by synthesis. We are responsible for the evolution of our theory and how we cultivate or fail to cultivate the capacity to integrate what is of value to our work from BOTH Freud's admonition against self-disclosure and Henry's, dare I say, demand for it.

I think we do ourselves and each other a disservice when we react to something before we fully understand it, as I am laying it out here, considering the rest of the story. Is mutual understanding of the proponent of the thesis and antithesis a valuable circumstance for eventually reaching a synthesis? It is important to understand that an antithesis in not yet a complete innovation. I believe innovation happens at the point of synthesis. Adaptive change is not just a matter of making things "right". It is more complex than that, something I think we understand well in our work with our patients who strive to have something different than they grew up with only to in some form recreate those circumstances, sometimes by simply doing the opposite. This is due to not fully understanding or working through their history. If we just strive to simply correct the past, we just make the winners, losers and the losers, winners, a recipe for the next power shift. Change on the surface does not address the important considerations deeper down.

Now I want to give Henry's essay more due consideration. To begin, I am presuming that he does not fully understand contemporary ego psychology. I have two reasons. First, he depicts it as a "Mad Men" like theory practiced by white male psychoanalysts smoking cigarettes. This is a caricature that I do not believe represents us today. Secondly, he appreciates but does not believe Glen Gabbard and Thomas Ogden's advocacy for open engagement with explaining why. He is depicting the thesis he is representing the antithesis of, in a manner that feel dismissive to me. I propose, as a thought experiment, a conversation between Henry and one or both of these present-day psychoanalysts (we'll just skip the Mad Men) where he can ask them more about how they apply what they are laying out and they can ask Henry questions about what considerations he applies in determining how much, what and when to disclose to a patient.

Or actually I can ask him that question here. Henry, what considerations do you apply in determining how much, what and when to disclose to a patient? What do you understand the purpose to be? I am suspicious of the idea that self-dis-closure in and of itself creates a real relationship that is ther-apeutic. How to you track or evaluate that?

I want to add more about Henry's depiction of the thesis he opposes. He declares that "(a)nalysts are creatures of habit and often prisoners of theory and basic assumptions" and asks us to "consider and acknowledge that most training in psychoanalysis doesn't encourage thinking that is critical of received wisdom about either the theory of that institute and certainly not the importance of technical rules..." I presume he has experienced this in interaction with one or more an-alysts and/or training institutes, but I object to the general-ization. What I believe is at the heart of analytic thinking, the very act of being an analyst, is critical thinking. This is what floats my boat. And I have not been constrained in my ten-dency to think critically over the course of my training and engagement in the analytic community.

I see our plethora of theoretical and technical innovations **as** evidence of our capacity for critical thinking. I think I align with Henry that something prevents integration of this pro-gression. So, we have Freud's original thesis (within which he made many iterations), many antitheses and very limited syntheses. Synthesis does take work. Both work by all the in-dividuals involved and work in the form of interaction among the proponents of the thesis and the antithesis. I think it is hard but necessary to understand something one disagrees with. This is not an easy task, but we appreciate the value of it as, for example, we can see our patients beginning to relate to their parents more as fully fleshed out people (I was go-ing to say whole objects but thought better of it). The latter takes being fully engaged with one's opponent without being loaded for bear. Killing the other idea can mean losing some-thing that is essential for, as I see it, real innovation and sta-ble adaptive change.

Over the decades of theoretical conflicts and developments, much of which Henry spans in his essay, it seems to me that we have had trouble coming up with a shared language and understanding. The trauma of the times (two world wars, the Great Depression, the holocaust, etc.), narcissistic needs, misunderstandings, the impact of psychoanalysis spreading across the globe and mixing with different cultures are just some of the contributing factors I can brainstorm. I am sure there many more.

As I entered the field with no bones, in the form of previous exposure, and so no bones to pick, my reaction to all the different theoretical branches has been different. I do not have any trouble seeing Melanie Klein and Donald Winnicott's contributions as additive. They address stages of development that Freud did not fully get to, and I would say therefore did not see a way to treat the problems that could arise because of disruptions during these phases. As Freud strove to solidify his discoveries, I can appreciate his protectiveness of his theories and ideas about technique, particularly those that are difficult to consider, think infantile sexuality. Even as Freud discovered something new and left a previous idea behind, I do not think that he dismissed it completely. I would describe it as something like the old sofa that we relegated to the basement when we got a new one, but that continues to be an important piece of furniture. At some point the "old" sofa may prove it's worth as an antique and be the center piece of redecorating.

For many years now we have treated what was commonly termed widening scope cases—those who became more likely to seek our care based on their need, insurance constraints, and changes in what is popular for the bulk of the worried well. As a part of this transition, we modified our techniques whether we declared it in opposition to tradition (original thesis) or kept quiet about it as Freud seemed to have with his own modifications when he was talking about general technique. His generosity, in terms of openness about the variation in his technique, can be seen in what could be considered his widening scope cases.

Language is, of course, a major human achievement and, in its lack of capacity to fully represent what it is symbolizing, holds the seeds of many human problems. As a tool for connecting with each other in a meaning making manner, it has launched so much of our development, as individuals and communities, aided us in our survival and been a means whereby we create more and more advanced art and technology. But when we trust our words too much, they can confuse or disrupt interaction more than they facilitate it. When we are working at the abstract level of theory, I think this is amplified. I assume that most of you, as clinicians and/or patients, will relate to my experience of a meaningful and rich metaphor becoming stale. I clearly remember an instance in my training analysis where my analyst objected to my continued use of a phrase we had arrived at in an emotionally intense moment in the work. I was upset at first and then could clearly see that I was trying to hang onto that past moment, to use it as a shortcut to get back to the experience of an affectively meaningful discovery. And as an analyst, I have caught myself trying to get the work going by using the same word or phrase that has been very useful in the past. I can feel that I'm trying to use a shortcut, not the kind that gets us there quickly and elegantly, but one that threatens to get us lost or there before we are ready to come together in a new shared space.

Keeping our theoretical language fresh is a challenge as well. I can easily see it when technical language is used too much as a shortcut. It tends to grow stale and contribute more to misunderstanding than understanding—resulting in our losing real contact with each other and/or the juice of our ideas.

Henry argues that there is a lack of proof for conservative theories while at the same time not presenting proof for his own. I think I can read between the lines that he has had experience in his consulting room with analysands who presented that they had been harmed by conservative, anonymous analysts. If this is the case, it may act as a kind of proof to him. I can appreciate that with the constraints of confidentiality, he is limited in terms of self-disclosure and therefore elaborating his proof. Unfortunately, his proof on that basis cannot serve as proof for me and I think it complicates reaching synthesis.

That said I have had or witnessed encounters where an analysis is privileged by the analyst over real-life considerations that I found objectionable and a lack of openness to new ideas and new or younger professionals that I found off-putting—particularly at national meetings. I will also note here that one instance of offense is due to Henry's characterization of nonphysicians as not being bound by consideration of the effectiveness of their work in helping their patients. As a mental health counselor by licensure, I am curious about the basis of this opinion and can say unequivocally that it is not my training, view or ethic to ignore what my patients say about how they are doing.

These instances support Henry's characterizations of our field as stuck in the past. I can imagine the impact on someone who's predominant experience was of this kind. I have found plenty that has been otherwise generative in my engagement in the field. How do we work this through and embrace the future we are inexorably moving toward and remaining sufficiently grounded in what our past has to offer.

As a function of a period of decline in interest in psychoanalysis that Henry described, I was recruited for training, teaching and becoming a training analyst. Two waivers were requested and obtained for my training. The first was to train as a master's level counselor and the second was to be able to conduct my training analysis, after the first nearly two years, by telephone. These occurred in 2004 and 2006 respectively. I graduated earlier than I would have when my institute adopted the Columbia model (alternative requirement for cases under training consultation). My immersion (amount of post graduate experience conducting analysis) was considered with flexibility by the committee that evaluated me for a training analyst appointment. I realize that I have benefited from the timing of my entry into our field.

To make my contribution to a dialectic dialogue on anonymity versus self-disclosure, I would like to draft my answer to the question I posed to Henry. What do I use to consider how anonymous, abstinent or neutral to be with any given patient at any given moment? The first place I went is to the question about my role as a good object and/or bad object. This can address whether I desire to be a good object (providing more direct help as I see it) at this moment and what that is about in me or whether having a bad object experience (allowing for the emergence or continuation of negative/painful responses to me) might be helpful for my patient in some way. But given our loaded language, my use of these terms may be less helpful rather than more. I could resort to gratifying versus frustrating but that is likely to be even more trouble.

As I am challenged to think about what I mean when I use these terms, I am reminded of how I contextualize these questions in my understanding of development as I try to assess whether my patient can benefit from me being directly or indirectly helpful. This is a judgement that parents are making all the time about different things over the course of their child's development. A classic example is a parent's response to a child, who is learning to walk and falls or how to manage a tantrum. There are important considerations whether to jump in to help versus standing by and even enduring our anxiety or their attacks.

In any given moment, I use my best judgment, see how it goes and together my patient and I try to make sense of it. I am working on my own and with my patient to understand their developmental needs and provide an atmosphere that facilitates their growth. In moments of these kinds of consideration, I find myself working hard to be available. By that I mean striving to be available to the patient, able to not know what is happening (against Henry's stereotype), available to my inner experience and available in that moment. Of course, there is considerable variation in my capacity for this in any given session or moment within a session. But having cultivated this kind of focus and felt the benefit of it in the work, I trust it more and more. This is what I believe our real relationship is built on regardless of how much I self-disclose about my life and/or my internal experience. I think it is the life of the work that I share with each patient that is the basis for our real relationship, the kind of open relationship that Henry is advocating. It is within this that we work to explicate the impact of past experience for both of us on our ability to be together and tackle the question(s) at hand.

I want to share a case example to illustrate what I believe are the complexities around self-disclosure that need to be considered both at the outset and as the work proceeds. During the mid phase of a four-time-per-week analysis there were several instances where I was feeling particularly warm toward my patient. I ended up expressing this in two different ways with two different results, both meaningful and complex.

The first expression was in the form of what I intended as a gift. We had done some painful exploratory work and he had also referenced aspects of his own professional work. Since I knew that he was interested in psychoanalysis and there is a psychoanalytic term to describe both of these kinds of work, I told him the term. His response in that moment was positive and nothing else came of it until several weeks later as we were talking about the second expression of warmth. This time at the end of a rich session where I felt I better understood his experience in adolescence, I said the following: "When your mom insisted and frantically told you about the girls' side of sexual experiences, you felt she was saying to you that she didn't trust you and that she wasn't able to see you as a sensitive, thoughtful young man."

The next session was the last appointment before I would be gone for a week, followed by his planned absence for another week. To begin the session, I came to get him in the waiting area from the hall outside my suite instead of from my office like I usually would. He said, "I was expecting a client. I was surprised." I asked him what that was like. He states that: "It took me off guard and I had to slow down." I asked from what and he said eagerly: "From jumping up to be at your beckon call." I replied, "That's a big thing that's always there." He confirmed this and stated, "I won't see you for a couple of weeks." I said, "That's right." After a pause, he responded, "Which is sad," and I said, "Can you say more?" He went on to say, "I'll miss you and our time together. It's grounding when I get to come here. I feel like I'll be fine. It was nice to hear what you said at the end of the session yesterday. I wrote it down. That I'm sensitive and thoughtful. That essentially, I can figure stuff out. It felt like that came from a nice place. It felt real and I trusted it. Even though it wasn't direct I took it as coming from you." I said, "You took it that I saw those things." To which he said, "It helped." He talked about multiple intense emotional experiences at work and in his personal life with the focus on being able to tolerate these things without having to control or fix them. I asked him why he thought that my statement got in as well as it did the previous day. He said, "Huh—a couple of things. It felt real. I'm sensitive and you acknowledged it. You didn't say toughen up. You showed that I could handle it.... You acknowledged that I am a young man. I just turned 30. I was young when I was a kid. It was the feeling that I have a lot in front of me and I don't have to figure it out. It was the trust piece. That you trusted that I am able. You say it all the time by being present the way that you are. At times I get pissed, the times when it feels like you encroach on that."

I ask how so. He answered, "Like the time that you said (here he names the term I used), I experience that as not trusting, that you were saying it needed a label." I said, "It's like I thought you didn't know something." He came back with, "I wanted to hit you with neurological research." I asked him if he could stay with it. He responded, "Are we really going to do terms, I can kick your ass." I kept with the theme: "It was like I pulled out the boxing gloves." He replied, "Yeah, really, really, what you're 5'7", 5'5". Are you fucking kidding me—you don't have a prayer. You don't know how fucked you are. Maybe I'll hold back." I continued: "You could totally crush me." He did the same: "Yes, fuck you for putting me in that position. I don't want to do that at all. That's what I got from my mom, you, my boss—Be gentle'. I don't need someone to box with. I don't need you to toughen me up. I know."

I said, "You've been training for this all your life." He replied, "Totally—fuck that." I said,

"You've been holding back, but you don't have to." And he continued: "No, I can let it fly. I can crush people, people I love. I hate that they experience it as so mean. I'll be relentless. You may beat me up this round, but I've been training for this my whole life.

Even if I cry, I endure more than most people. You better look out. It's why I came here. I'm using it as boxing practice. I'm gonna find all the moves that can be done to me. If I get out into the world, I've already trained. Good luck using this against me."

I commented, "So I've helped with the training." He confirmed that I had inadvertently. As he began to wind down and after a pause, he wondered if he is tired then said, "I'm not tired, I know I'm not—I kind a love it." I responded, "You're not ready to let it go," and he said, "No, what would be there?" I repeat, "What would be there?" He answered, "The soft old me at the farmers market getting flowers and fruit to cook in a straw hat and looking like such a pussy." Here we began work to integrate other parts of him and his response to my leaving, which ended up at the end of the session being soft and kind.

As analysts, we have all kinds of experience in our work with our patients. In this set of papers, we are wrestling with whether and how to disclose them. In this clinical example with J, my different forms of expression (the presentation of an analytic term as a gift to express tenderness and a displaced and indirect expression of trust) were experienced very differently by J from each other and over time. While we have in this example his ability to read my sentiment in both instances in the moment, I expressed them as I intended in one instance consciously and the other likely preconsciously, the gift of a psychoanalytic term did not remain in him as it had been received.

I think the important part is not what I initiated but what J did with them and then how we were able to establish and preserve space for him to express/self-disclose himself. As he put it, I communicated more to him by how I was with him than by what I tried to say to him. I think change happens via engagement rather than self-disclosure. I rely mainly on my patients' disclosure to do the work. My work is to provide the space for it, to hear and understand it, to allow it to engage me, consciously and unconsciously.

Part of my point is that I am working to be as present as I can be, bringing as much of my whole self as I am able. This is a kind of presence/expression/disclosure that makes space for my patient's experience and capacity to be present/express/ disclose/experience and I think grow. As you can see from the example, I am not silent, but I am judicious about what I contribute from myself. I find that the value of my active presence in the form of talking varies from patient to patient and with each patient from moment to moment. I do not think that who I am, in terms of disclosing, helps my patients as much as what I provide. As result I can be quite different in each treatment or over the course of a treatment. Saying more can turn to saying less and vice versa.

As an analytic clinician I think that we need the capacity to self-disclose and to refrain from self-disclosure. This allows us greater freedom to consider what might work in any given situation and requires us to consider the benefits and costs of each option. Along these lines, I think our work is ultimately both a shared endeavor and at the same time I am working as a professional with clear responsibilities. They in fact include my need to make determinations about interventions I use and whether they are effective. That is the case self-disclosure or remaining anonymous, abstinent and neutral. In our clinical work to only be a real person in a real relationship, to my mind, is akin to breaking the incest taboo in the context of the family. It is our challenge to honor this professional responsibility and, at the same time, the essential integrity of those we work with. I heard Henry give a nod to this in his criticism of non-physicians I referenced above.

Grace exhorts us to think critically, particularly about ourselves, instead of reacting. I don't think that we get any easy directions in this work. To disclose or not to disclose? I believe we must always take up this question and wrestle with its answer with each patient and in each moment. Additionally, I believe our real relationship with our patients is not based on what we disclose to them so much as it is based on what we experience together. I agree with Henry that being anonymous, not answering questions, is powerful, but answering them is also powerful.

We must conduct the hard work of determining what to try or realize what we tried before we knew it consciously, see how it goes and proceed from there with the same level of uncertainty, agonizing, creativity, spontaneity or impulsivity, as the case may be, and live a good amount of life with our patients on the path to seeing where this analysis will take both of us.

I'd like to close with my last personal story about relating across differences. I grew up visiting family ranches in Wyoming. This experience remained a home base for me during many moves over my growing years. I love riding horses, but I am not very good at it. I am also, most of the time the only Democrat around and this emerged during President Obama's first term, when I was called out about it. This did not prompt an extensive debate. Although I would indulge in that with one cousin when we were one on one, there was not much point in a larger group since no one was going to convince anyone of anything in that context. So, I was happy to stand my ground proudly and leave it at that when my cousin's teenage son in an ominous tone talked about there being some Democrats in the valley and he knew where they lived. I did not know him well enough to have any idea whether he was just trying to get my goat or expressing a sincere and dark sentiment.

One evening on this visit when I was out for a ride with my aunt and my cousin's teenage daughter—Emma, my horse hit his back leg on a metal culvert and was limping as we galloped into the barnyard. I felt awful! I didn't know how badly he was hurt. To make matters worse a woman from Texas who sells horses was there visiting and she was ranting and raving about mistreating horses as Emma and her set to treating the wound. Emma reassured me quietly on the side that it wasn't a big deal, but I was not relieved. Added to all of this was the fact that everyone was gathered at the main house, something I did not always have to encounter. I did not want to walk in there, but I was no help to my injured horse, so in I went. The oddest thing happened. My uncle who listened to Rush Limbaugh daily and was the one that asked my dad what happened to me (that's how he called me out), responded to me announcing myself as the horse "hurter" by saying something about President Obama.

I do not remember what he said about Obama but suddenly I was ready for a fight. I noticed my internal change immediately and realized he had said that to free me from my guilt and the fury of a woman from Texas oddly enough named Hillary. My gratitude was expressed as I was able to just grin at him across the room and the conversation settled into its usual course. Better yet my horse was just fine. Our profound political difference was no match for the care and concern he had and adeptly expressed at a difficult moment for me. We knew each other as people first and that allowed for a difference to be a means to treat my wound in this case.

I am glad that we are having this kind of discussion since, I hope that along with hashing out controversies, we get to know each other better along with having a chance to hone our ideas. It seems to me that things are changing within psychoanalysis. I have had the fortune to be spared the traumatic experiences of many having to do with admission to training, graduation, certification (it was hard, but I found it to be a truly analytic and mutual critical thinking process) and being appointed as a TA even while my institute is working on dismantling this institution while trying to maintain what it adds. As I understand it the William Alanson White Institute that Henry mentioned was ejected from the American Psychoanalytic Association rejoined APsA in recent years. We just voted on expanded membership, and we have begun to benefit from the hard work and the wisdom of the Holmes Commission. One of the notable features they included in their report at the national meetings this year was the importance of having a process that addresses institutional prejudice and exclusion. I think we need new processes for multiple purposes.

As he closes his essay, Henry declares that if we allow ourselves the freedom to be ourselves, our patients will be able to maintain the growth that they gain to a degree that "far exceeds" traditional analysis. This feels to me akin to that idea that just being anonymous facilitates the emergence of a transference neurosis that can be worked through via interpretation. Both descriptions seem too simplistic to me.

I haven't found a way to not be myself in the intense engagement that is a part of our work whether I'm particularly self-disclosing or not. My challenge is to know myself and my patient as well as our relationship as much as I am able and for us to uncover and experience our shared humanity. This is not an easy process. As I have wrestled with many aspects of technique and worked to apply my own capacity to use dialectical thinking to the many contributors in our literature and meetings, I hope I have gleaned something of value from each. I find that each patient and in many ways each session evolves in unique ways. And while I think all this preparation is critical, ultimately it allows us to be more available and engaged. So, to both agree and disagree with Henry, I will close by saying that I believe it is our humanity that heals.

Final Note: Having completed a full draft of this prior to the Spring 2023 controversy in APsA, I find there is more I feel compelled to add as I finalize what I have to say here. The hope and promise of the work and change that was occurring leading up to the eruption was palpable but not as close at hand as it seemed. Controversial discussions have abounded in the course of events from that time until today in the context of a deeply painful history and present, and profoundly traumatic events. I believe that we have much to do to truly understand each other and find better ways to live together in equity and harmony. I hope that we will continue the labor of fulfilling the vision of the Holmes Commission Report and each of our purest desires to be a complete community.

References

Boggs, J. & Boggs, G.L. (1974). *Revolution and Evolution in The Twentieth Century*. New York: Monthly Review Press.

Dickens, C. (1707). *A Tale of Two Cities*. Garden City, NY: Dover Publications, 1998.

Durant, W. & Durant, A. (1968). *The Lessons of History*. New York: Simon & Schuster, 2010.

Chapter 5
Therapeutic Action, A Hypothesis

Edward Nersessian

In a number of recent presentations (Nersessian) it has been asserted that psychoanalytic theory is grounded on concepts that are derived from a neurophysiology that is out-dated. Freud's basic tenets some of which continue to be the backbone of psychoanalytic theory are over 100 years old. Interestingly, and perhaps surprisingly, a similar point was made recently about neuroscience by Peter Stern in *Science* in the October 27, 2017, issue. He stated: "Could it be that we are interpreting our data with outdated concepts? Most of the dominant concepts in present-day neuroscience, after all, were developed 50 to more than 100 years ago."

It is therefore essential, for those of us who have been actively engaged in psychoanalysis to begin the process of revisiting our basic concepts from a more modern vantage point and to try to put forward hypothesis that attempt to explain the efficacy of the psychoanalytic therapeutic approach.

Prior to presenting one such hypothesis, it will perhaps be useful to briefly review the arguments questioning some of the basic concepts.

Brief review of the fundamental tenets of Psychoanalysis

There may be some differing opinions as to what constitute the fundamental concepts or tenets of psychoanalytic theory, at least as developed by Freud. We have selected the following for the purpose of the present arguments: The dynamic unconscious; repression; drives; pleasure principle and infantile sexuality.

These foundational notions of psychoanalytic theory were developed quite early in Freud's career but continued to be dominant despite the revisions he brought to bear on his hypothesis. The 1923 reworking of the model of the mind presented in the paper "The Ego and the Id," while introducing important modifications to more classical ideas, nevertheless maintained the primacy of the tenets listed above. What is, however, essential to keep in mind regarding the 1923 revision is that it cut ties with neurophysiology that is to say with the brain. Psychoanalytic theory became a pure theory of the mind and therefore unconstrained by neurophysiologic principles. It also gave free rein to theorizing and from that point on Freud and his followers proposed various notions that were based on scant verifiable evidence. Psychoanalysis became an independent field with an increasingly complex set of notions that were based on the observations and consequent theorizing of its practitioners without any other scientific validation.

While developing hypotheses which can be properly tested, which is essential in any scientific field, the constraints imposed by the "one on one" confidential relationship of the psychoanalytic situation forecloses the possibility of testing the observations and subsequent theorizing generated in the mind of the psychoanalyst in the clinical situation. Unable to apply regular research protocols, psychoanalysis, over the period of its development gradually and unavoidably became an ever expanding theory made up of opinions of individual practitioners, where the only consensus to arrive at was through other practitioners agreeing with the opinion and its elaborations.

Returning to the fundamental tenets, originally roughly based on the neurophysiology of the day as described in "Project for a Scientific Psychology", they became relatively quickly independent of any connection to the brain even though and paradoxically, the ideas that were somewhat based on the physiology of the day remained central to psychoanalytic theory and some remain so to this day.

Again, the fundamental hypothesis we have chosen to examine in the present work are the following;

1. Repression and the dynamic unconscious
2. Pleasure-unpleasure principle, briefly
3. Drives, briefly
4. Infantile sexuality and psychosexual phases of development.

Undoubtedly, the idea of a dynamic unconscious is at the center of psychoanalytic thinking, but Freud did not begin with the notion of an unconscious. Rather, he and Breuer were first led to the concept of defense and repression by their clinical experiences and observations. The dominant notion of the time, which was shared by Freud, held that memories left a permanent trace; accordingly, if one did not remember, it was because the memory was prevented from being recalled, that is to say, it was defended against or repressed and therefore was unconscious. To make the memory become conscious, a resistance needed to be overcome. This led Freud to use a technique he had learned from Bernheim, who used it to bring forth memories from periods of somnambulism with the pressure on the head, and from this, the notion of resistance became central to his thinking.

In addition, since Breuer and Freud further observed that many of the memories their patients were not revealing had to do with sexual matters, including adolescent crushes and the like, they assumed that repression was keeping these prohibited sexual ideas out of consciousness and that sexuality was also central to psychopathology. Parenthetically, originally Freud did not believe that normal people had an unconscious, only hysterics, but that view rapidly changed.

Over time, as Freud's clinical work advanced and he invented free association, the theory of repression became central in neurosogenesis in general and was not limited to hysteria. Furthermore, through his self-analysis, he discovered the importance of childhood experiences which then led him to the notion of repression of infantile memories and wishful impulses. Eventually, the notion of primal repression needed to be added to justify that not only were wishes and thoughts pushed back but that they were also being pulled, that is to say attracted, into the UCS, an idea closely tied to the of concept of infantile amnesia. By 1914, when he published the metapsychological papers, psychoanalytic theory had become much more nuanced and sophisticated and herein, in the paper on "The Unconscious," Freud offered a classification of unconscious mental phenomena that delineates the "dynamic unconscious" as the place where repressed impulses and memories reside.

In as much as repression gives rise to the dynamic unconscious, the conceptual problems apparent in both are not only related but synonymous, as we will now enumerate:

1. Creating a theory of repression based on the patient's resistance to reveal is a flawed thesis grounded in a weak argument. The patient may simply be consciously withholding in order to avoid a painful emotion.

2. The original optimism of Freud and Breuer about lifting of repression was not justified. The patients revealing their thoughts under hypnosis or pressure on the forehead did not show consistent improvement.

3. In a given situation what decides which part of a wish, memory or experience is repressed? The entity Freud called the ego from early on in his work, and which he

later made in part unconscious, creates a whole set of theoretical conundrums if it is to be founded on the underlying biology.

4. The notions of repression, defense and resistance brings up the concept of forces and inevitably raises the issue of the nature and source of these forces, but there is no evidence to support the contention that any such forces exist. While it is possible to talk of inhibition or even suppression in brain activity, it is difficult to justify the notion of force. Moreover, in developing the notion of cathexis and counter-cathexis, Freud went even further out on the limb by stating that these forces are not only involved in keeping ideas associated with instinctual impulses out of consciousness, but they are also involved in pushing them into consciousness. Given that the ideas are assumed to obtain their force by being associated to the instinctual impulse, then what is the source of the anti-cathexis? This issue was never comfortably resolved by Freud, and it does not correspond at all to what is presently known about brain function. In fact, it can be said that the concept is based on a metaphor with no counterpart in reality.

5. Most importantly, the notion of repression implies discreet entities, be it a discreet memory or a specific wish. In the 1914 paper on the unconscious Freud states, "Unconscious ideas continue to exist after repression as actual structures in the system uncs." However, (as we know from memory research) wishes and memories are in constant interaction with other wishes and memories, this interaction moves both forwards and backwards, as present and past experiences influence and are influenced by other contents of the mind/brain creating networks. Therefore, there are no structures or discrete entities such as Freud delineated, rather, there are increasingly complex networks.

6. This notion of discrete entities is also problematic in relation to Freud's idea of the return of the repressed, which implies that one of these objects or discreet entities in the mind can enter consciousness in a circumscribed way and can be recognized as such. Instead, we know that all experiences, including traumatic or emotionally relevant ones, are always present in the mind. They exist today because of the effect they have had on subsequent experiences; they are embedded in them. To the degree that any experience is in interaction with other past and future experiences, it is difficult to justify that recalling a specific event can alter all the subsequent effects of the original experience.

A very brief clinical example to underscore illustrate this point: A 77-year-old man is in conflict with his wife over her wish to travel to foreign countries. He states, "My first foreign travel was to Vietnam when I was 19. I was crawling down VC tunnels with a flame thrower. When I made it back to the US I literally kissed the ground. Those memories are always with me and they prevent me from leaving this country again." He certainly seems conscious of the trauma, but that does not alleviate the anxiety.

Before further examination of these points, a few very general comments about autobiographic memory and contemporary research on memory may be useful. Memory, which was Freud's primary interest as opposed to semantic memories or procedural memory, is now known from a neuropsychological and neuroscientific point of view to be distorted and inaccurate, and at times even totally fabricated from pieces of memory and experience in part due to processes of consolidation and reconsolidation and contextualization. Accordingly, in this schema, autobiographic memory is malleable; anything that is recalled is a re-construction that may or not be factual. While much of this work on the micro-biology, genetics and epigenetics of memory, as well as on consolidation and re-consolidation is performed on animals and the findings may or may not be applicable or valid for humans, it represents a potential area for fruitful collaborative work between researchers and psychoanalysts. Laboratory research is necessarily constrained by the limitations of its subjects and by conscribed methods of data collection, and certainly, it is clear that animal brains lack the complexity and layering that allows for the advanced capacities of human memory and that the human environment is infinitely more complex than any pared-down conditioning experiment in the lab. As psychoanalysts whose subjects of study can and do speak volumes, we are uniquely situated to observe and report on the on-going changes in memory functioning that are seen in the psychoanalytic setting.

Returning to the evolution of Freud's ideas and to recapitulate them, his clinical observations of patients led to the view that memories were being kept out of awareness; consequently, he determined that they must be forcefully kept out of consciousness. This then led to the next inference, that of the concept of the dynamic unconscious. It is important not only to note how Freud moved so easily from observation to inference to established theory but even more important for our focus today, we must recognize that these concepts of repression and the dynamic unconscious are based on two outdated ideas: one is the notion of energy, flow of energy and force, and the other is the view that memory is made up of well delineated entities, with all the components, affective, sensory and cognitive being prevented by some force from entering consciousness.

A second bedrock of psychoanalytic thinking that bears re-examination in the light of 21st century science is the pleasure-unpleasure principle. This idea originated with the constancy principle, which was already introduced in the Project and which gradually assumed a position of central importance in psychoanalytic theory. Even though the idea was modified in "Beyond the Pleasure Principle" with the introduction of the death instinct, the basic principle remained and remains important in psychoanalysis. For Freud, the principle had first to do with the accumulation of excitation that was perceived as unpleasant and the discharge as pleasant. Some of his thinking was based on knowledge of sexual arousal as it leads to orgasm. He considered the state of arousal as un-pleasurable and as leading to a need for discharge in order to restore homeostasis, and he enlarged this observation to encompass the realm of mental functioning. Again, Freud started with an observation and transmuted it into a principle of mental functioning, in the process conflating observation with explanation. Pleasure in orgasm can be consciously experienced and readily observed, but how does it follow that the mind is regulated by the need to balance pleasure and un-pleasure?

This U-shaped tube concept of pleasure-un-pleasure was very much part of 19th century science and was further advanced in our field by Charles Brenner. But while homeostasis remains an important concept in physiology, to my mind it does not apply to pleasure and un-pleasure. As any clinician has observed, arousal in itself can be pleasurable and there are people who enjoy maintaining arousal for long periods of time because of the pleasure derived from this state: Tantric sexual practices being one example. Additionally, pleasure today is not a simple, unitary concept; there are many varieties of pleasure, complex interactions exist between pleasure and un-pleasure., and some pleasurable experiences may have no connection to un-pleasure. For example, the delight of listening to a piece of music or the joy of seeing a work of art cannot be logically connected to un-pleasure. Instead, like any affective phenomena, pleasure and un-pleasure are conscious, whereas any regulatory mechanism is an integral part of how the brain/mind works.

In this presentation, we will focus on infantile sexuality and the psycho-sexual stages of development and will not delve in detail into the problem of aggression nor the thorny subject of instincts and drives which was so central to Freud's view of the working of the mind. Suffice it to say that some attempts have been made to find correspondence between Freud's Id and drives and the seeking system described by

Jaak Panksepp, but to us, these efforts have been unconvincing. A more intriguing line of inquiry that does not rely on the concept of drives comes from the work of Joseph LeDoux who delineates regulatory circuits, the instantiation of which leads to specific goals. He proposes five such circuits: fluid regulation, nutrition, thermoregulation, reproduction and defense that are essential for survival. We hope that this and other such lines of research may eventually yield useful data for our understanding of human behavior rather than the ill defined notion of drives, which if related or identical to instincts is on the level of observation and therefore is too broad. The Id, on the other hand, the dark territory, as Freud himself called it, is an even more difficult hypothetical entity to correlate with anything known about neural activity.

So, turning to infantile sexuality which was already widely discussed and reported in late nineteen century, we see that well-before the "Three Essays on Sexuality." Freud was already interested in childhood sexuality and erotogenic zones (a term already in use by Binet and others) as revealed in his correspondence with Fleiss. In letter #52, written in 1896, he states, "Hysteria is not repudiated sexuality, it is repudiated perversion. Furthermore, behind this lies the idea of abandoned EROTOGENIC ZONES. That is to say, during childhood sexual release would seem to be obtainable from very many parts of the body, which at a later time are only able to release the 28-day anxiety substance and not the others." It is not possible to determine how these ideas germinated in his thinking, but perhaps the following quote from letter 75 written in 1897 to Fliess offers a clue:

"I wrote to you once in the summer (letter 64) that I was going to find the source of normal sexual repression (morality, shame etc.) and then for a long time failed to find it. Before the holidays I told you that the most important patient for me was myself; and then suddenly, after I came back from holidays, my self-analysis, of which there was no sign, started ahead. A few weeks ago (letter 72) came my wish that repression might be replaced by the essential thing lying behind it;

and that is what I am concerned with now. I have often suspected that something organic played a part in repression; I was able to once before tell you that it was a question of the abandonment of former sexual zones (Freud is referring to erotogenic zones) and I was able to add that I had been pleased at coming at a similar idea in Moll."

By way of explanation, Albert Moll was a Berlin doctor who was part of a group of physicians considered to be sexologists. These men espoused an idea rather prevalent in the nineteenth century that there was an association between sexual problems and physical disorders. Freud clearly belonged in this group, although he and Moll actively disagreed and even disliked each other. From a historical perspective, it is evident that at that particular point in time in the late 19th century, those—including Freud—who accepted the so-called sexual theory were actively seeking to find proof linking the etiology of certain physical illnesses to underlying sexual disturbances. Further underscoring the legitimacy of this sexual science or Sexualwissenschaft, the journal "Zeitschrift fur Sexualwissenschaft," was launched in 1908 by Magnus Hirschfield. Once again, Freud was part of the scientific zeitgeist, but he took a decisive turn when he began to look more specifically for the sexual genesis of psychopathology. As we know, this shift in focus was also influenced by his studies with Charcot and by Charcot's eventual categorization of hysteria as psychological, as well as by his collaborations and publications with Joseph Breuer.

Freud's focus on sexuality did not develop in a vacuum, and given the predominance of ideas about the importance of sexuality in both physical and mental functioning, it undoubtedly influenced the discoveries he made in his self-analysis. According to the editors of the *Standard Edition,* "Three Essays on the Theory of Sexuality" stands alongside the "Interpretation of Dreams" as Freud's most momentous work.

There is no doubt that it impacted psychoanalytic thinking in a continuous way for the next hundred years and continues to do so, for some, even today. These essays helped to explain not only pathology but also character formation and entered into the realm of public discourse in myriad ways, sometimes in a salutary manner. Think, for example, of the changes in the ways we understand childhood and in how we approach child rearing that have been the result of the wide-spread dissemination of Freud's thinking.

The importance that Freud attributed to infantile sexuality cannot be underestimated. In the "Three Essays," he describes three important phases of sexual development in the child with relation to the progression of masturbation from infancy to early childhood to adolescence. Regarding the second phase, which he ascribed to beginning around age 4, he stated the following:

"The second phase of infantile sexuality may assume a variety of forms which can only be determined by a precise analysis of individual cases. But all its details leave behind the deepest unconscious impressions in the subjects memory, determine the development of his character, if he is to remain healthy, and the symptomatology of his neurosis, if he is to fall ill after puberty. In the latter case we find that this sexual period has been forgotten and that the conscious memories that bear witness to it have been displaced."

This is a sweeping claim—that masturbation in early childhood is strenuously repressed and that this repression, which he calls infantile amnesia, determines future character development and psychopathology.

Unfortunately, however, as a reading of the "Three Essays" reveals today, there was no solid data on which all this was based. Freud's data on erogenous zones, which was part of the sexual science of the day, and on the notion of component instincts were derived from knowledge about adult's perverse sexual practices as well as from such mundane observations of his day such the pleasure of kissing and anal intercourse and the sensitivity of the buccal and anal mucosa. Information obtained from adults in analysis was interpolated and applied to children. Babies were hypothesized to derive pleasure in an autoerotic way from sucking the breast or their thumb, just as they were presumed to derive sexual pleasure from their bowel movements. For example, apropos of the anal zone under the heading "Masturbatory Sexual Manifestations" Freud wrote, "like the labial zone, the anal zone is well suited by its position to act as a medium through which sexuality may attach itself to somatic functions" (*St. Ed.* vii, pp. 185). The very bedrock of Freud's theory rested on parallels which were drawn between adult sexual thoughts and behaviors and the behaviors of the child. Not only does such a theory presume that the mind of the child functions in its most significant aspects like that of an adult, but the theory also attributes an exaggerated sense of agency to the child. For example, asserting that the baby holds back feces in order to then have more pleasure presumes that the baby is capable of thinking and that it is capable of controlling his/hers bodily functions.

Given the state of neurobiological knowledge in the first half of the 20th century and the central role of repression and defense in psychoanalytic theory, the notion of infantile amnesia and its role in neurosogenesis seemed plausible. It is only later that studies of brain development in infants determined the timetable for the maturation of specific parts of the brain, and this knowledge allows for an entirely different understanding of infantile amnesia as an artifact of the ontogenesis of brain development.

There is no doubt that we can see behaviors in children that appear sexual, and there is also no doubt that there is a degree of curiosity about sexuality in children beginning around the age of 4 or 5 and sometimes even earlier. But for us, the critical issue is how do we understand this and how do we determine what role, if any, it has in character development and psychopathology. To our mind, the question as to whether we can speak of sexual pleasure in children in a Freudian sense is an open one that requires unbiased investigation. For example, it has not been determined whether the brain circuits activated in children during thumb-sucking or bowel movements are the same as those activated in the adult during sexual arousal and pleasure, and any such investigations would have to take into account the vast differences between adult levels of sexual hormones and the very low sexual hormone levels of children.

But there is another critical point to consider when looking at children: how much of any behavior is biologically determined and only secondarily assumes mental content? Children's play, for example, is at least in part genetically determined and is not that different from playful behavior observed in other species. I am in no way claiming here that there is no learned behavior or play but only that it would be highly questionable to ascribe to such cross-species biologically driven behaviors a central and exclusive role in on-going character development and in the evolution of psychopathology. Freud was not bound by such strictures; as I mentioned earlier, in the first decades of the twentieth century, generalizations, speculations, and even contradictions were readily accepted in theorizing. And, since taking biologically determined phenomena and giving them psychological motivations did not strike scientists as problematic the way it would today, Freud could, with equanimity, assert in the paper "The Dissolution of the Oedipus Complex (*St. Ed.* Vol. xix, 1929, p. 179) the following: "Renunciation of the penis is not tolerated by the girl without some attempt at compensation. She slips—along the line of a symbolic equation, one might say—from the penis to a baby. Her Oedipus complex culminates in a desire, which is long retained, to receive a baby from her father as a gift—to bear him a child. One has the impression that the Oedipus complex is then gradually given up because this wish is never fulfilled. The two wishes—to possess a penis and a child—remains strongly cathected in the unconscious and help to prepare the female creature for her later sexual role." (The use of the word creature here is interesting. Is he extending his idea to animals?) None of the above assertions is based on data; rather, it is pure theorizing at a level which appears rather fanciful through today's lens. In fact, the same can be said about Freud's Oedipus complex. The data for this supposedly invariant phase of psychosexual development came from Freud's self-analysis during the writing of the "Interpretation of Dreams," although, there is some suggestion that it also may already have been part of the discourse of the sexologists of that time. Unfortunately, however, as a reading of the "Three Essays on Sexuality" reveals today, there was no solid data on which all this was based.

These scientific considerations are important, but more critical for psychoanalysis today are the negative consequences of this intense focus on erogenous zones and psychosexual development and phases, most especially on the Oedipal phase. It has led us to narrow our view of early development and to so constrict our line of inquiry as to prevent us from being at the forefront of research on how the brain/mind of humans comes to be. Now that there is no evidence to support any of the connections between psychopathology and the psychosexual phases of development, be it obsessive compulsive disorders, phobic disorders, depressive disorders, paranoia etc. which Freud, Karl Abraham and others proposed, as well as data showing that orientations such as homosexuality or various gender preferences appear to have other possible determinants, it would free up psychoanalytic thinking if we took a broader view and studied the various contributions to the growing mind in a nondualist way.

The above is not to in any way apply that today's neuroscience is capable of explaining all the complex phenomena which go into what we call mind, in fact we can not even fully explain consciousness and self consciousness at this point, but only to say that whatever we have learned in the past 40 to 50 years requires that we revise psychoanalytic theory completely. However, the reality is that while such a revision can be initiated, it can not be fully accomplished with data from today's neuroscience, in other words, we do not yet possess sufficient validated knowledge to be able to explain the mind and the working of the various parts as well as their integration.

With the above in mind, we would very tentatively and speculatively suggest a different way of looking at early development, one that does not rely upon psychosexual development. I propose three significant elements: The genetic, the epigenetic, which is gaining increasing importance, and the environmental. All three of these elements contribute in a proximate, moment-to-moment fashion to the gradual growth of the brain/mind. As the neuronal connections increase, the interaction with the parents and surrogates and the environment (in reciprocal action with the genetic and epigenetic factors) form the infants mind. Every step effects the next step and may even alter aspects of the previous step, thus making us the individuals that we are, like our parents and other important people of our early life, and yet distinctly different. In a previous work (Nersessian) it was suggested in a tentative way that one way to describe what happens is to consider that these many factors create dynamic templates, maps, networks or using a modern popular concept, algorithms that determine the way the individual thinks and feels and reacts. In other words, the individuals mind is comprised of these maps, which include both explicit and implicit resultants of experiences including emotions. It is, we think, evident that the earlier experiences in life when the mind/brain is developing have a singularly important role in later experiences and therefore are a determining factor in these algorithms. Understanding and dissecting these dynamic maps or algorithms would be, to our mind, one way of defining psychoanalytic work.

Long before this paper was conceptualized, one of the authors, when faced with a patient who required an explanation for how therapy works, would answer with this somewhat funny joke:

"A man enters a big, modern synagogue. He notices that all the regulars bow upon entering. He turns to the very old man next to him for an explanation for this unusual practice. The old man tells him that this congregation started out in 1927 in the basement of a tenement. The doorway was only 5 feet high and if you didn't duck, you would smack your head. And they kept doing it even in the new building. These people think they are bowing, but they are really ducking. All people make rational decisions, commensurate with their understanding, to deal with the people and issues of their early life. It works to some degree or other. But 25 years later you may be engaged in the same ducking and think it is bowing and not realize that it is completely unnecessary. Maybe through our looking at your life in detail you will be able to give up some of the ducking."

Transference can be understood as the living out of these algorithms in the context of a new situation which provides few clues of what is expected. The analyst is accepting, non-judgmental, curious and gives little guidance. The patient has maximal latitude to express and experience previously created algorithms while the analyst observes and comments upon them. For example, "I have noticed that sometimes when I begin to speak, your body tenses and your head cringes. You have described how your father playfully smacks the back of your head and it startles you."

The issue for the patient in analysis is that certain patterns or algorithms have created patterns of behavior and emotion that interfere with a successful and happy life. The analytic work on these networks, which are how the patient experiences herself and the world, brings about a particular degree of inner freedom with important consequences in the persons way of being in and experiencing the world.

A case example: A 45-year-old lawyer entered treatment because, "I want to get married and I can't." He was an only child, born to an American couple who worked for the State Department in various foreign countries. He described his family life as "wonderful, my parents were the best." He is good looking, athletic and successful. He has had numerous serious relationships with women but always finds a reason for not marrying them. The reasons are always different, seem to be reasonable, but he can see that they are rationalizations. Early development seemed to have been happy and within expected norms. But over time the therapy revealed a number of trouble spots. His father had never been able to stand up to his mother to express what he wanted and over time the relationship deteriorated badly. In all of his relationships with women, the patient repeated this pattern of his father's. The relationship would unravel as he felt more unfulfilled, he would emotionally withdraw and the woman would finally leave. His mother was experienced as very self involved and sure of herself.

The patient had no male friends. He was quite gregarious, athletic and had numerous friends until puberty when all his peers shot past him. He did not begin to grow or sexually develop until he was 18. From 13 to 18 he was the butt of continuous sadistic and humiliating pranks due to his childish appearance. The world became a dangerous place and his only safety was experienced with his family. This pattern continued until he sought treatment.

One could say that the following algorithm dominated his thinking and behavior:

The world will humiliate me. Friends will hurt me. I am only comfortable around my family. Even if I find a woman who seems to love me, it is impossible to negotiate or work out with her a viable relationship. And she will ultimately be interested in her own selfish needs.

All of these themes were painfully experienced in the transference and gradually analyzed.

Many experienced clinicians instinctively work in this manner, without resorting to concepts such as infantile sexuality or the Oedipus complex. Some clinicians seem to feel that they must "throw a bone" to such concepts, otherwise it is not real analysis. Certainly, many feel that such concepts must work their way into cases that are written up for various reasons. And as for memory, the bulk of the work in the above case was done in the here and now of the transference. Certainly, the patient frequently associated to past or long past experiences. But those memories were not the basis of interpretations.

According to the patient, the most helpful thing in the treatment was the ability to put his feelings BASED ON HIS EARLY EXPERIENCE into words and have his pain understood and accepted. The things that he spoke about were not newly uncovered memories. They were thoughts and feelings that he had never dared to speak about before. That the analyst heard him and still accepted him felt surprising and powerful.

To talk of experience raises the issue of memory and it may be useful here to briefly review our current understanding of memory, its types, its consolidation and its loss.

Since Freud and other psychoanalytic thinkers such as Ernst Kris, memory research has made important advances forward. The studies done on the patient HM by the neurosurgeon William Beecher Scoville and the neuropsychologist Brenda Miller were important in ushering in the progress made in memory research. Research that has benefitted from the contributions of Daniel Schacter, Larry Squire, Joseph LeDoux and many other prominent researchers in the field.

These studies have led, if not to a fuller understanding of memory, certainly to a classification of memory that has allowed for deeper appreciation of the types of memories that humans and other mammals rely on. This classification distinguishes broad categories of sensory memories, short term memories and long term memories. Psychoanalytic interest lies mostly, though not only, in long term memories and in particular in autobiographical memories. Briefly, long term memories are divided into Explicit and Implicit Memories. Explicit memories being conscious and implicit being unconscious. Included in implicit memories are procedural memories which have to do with procedures such as tying shoe laces. Declarative memories are explicit and they include episodic memories, which are memories of events and experiences, and semantic memories, which have to do with facts and concepts. Autobiographical memories, which are explicit memories, are what have traditionally interested psychoanalysts.

Recollection during psychoanalysis of repressed memories, whether through associations, dreams, or in response to interpretation has played an important role in psychoanalytic work from its beginning though the early period conviction in the curative value of the lifting of repression has taken backstage. Instead, an exploration in detail of certain memories and how they have been altered has become the therapeutic modality. In other words, psychoanalysis has asserted that the inaccuracies and even outright fabrications in autobiographic memory are significant because such alterations have been made for a reason, that memory distortions are tendentious, and their analysis helpful in understanding the important issues in the persons life. In the classical psychoanalytic way of thinking the distortions are the result of defensive activity motivated by unconscious forbidden wishes (Nersessian).

What we would propose at this time, however, is that memories, specifically autobiographic memories, and their distortions, whatever the reason for the distortions may be, while important, play a much smaller role in analytic treatment and that for the reasons we will describe.

In the late 19th century and through a good part of the twentieth, memory was seen as presence of islands in the mind (island of memory). This implied that they were circumscribed and resided in the mind/brain after being consolidated.

Important research by Alberini and others on consolidation and reconsolidation has shown the degree to which memories are modified through this process. The approach I am proposing tentatively here is that we include in our conception of memory the total effect of the event on the person, of which the memory is but a part.

When we look at our lives, we see continuity, a narrative which is more or less cohesive and which gives our self a sense of existence over a period of time usually from our childhood to the present. Even though these memories are most often not continuous, and the ones from our childhood are really like islands, we nevertheless develop a feeling of continuity and cohesion. In other words, we can build a story of our life. A story however, which not only is not always totally accurate (the inaccuracies of autobiographical memory have been well documented. However, more studies in the nature of the alterations and distortions are needed in order to better understand the reasons, perhaps multiple, for such alterations and their salience namely, whether there are essential elements of memories that are different from what occurred or less important details), but which, much more importantly, is not but a small part of the life we have lived. This is because who we are is based on our experiences, physical, sensory, mental, and explicit memory is only the foam on top of the ocean water. Experiences and experiencing is in fact who we are. In other words, our individual selves, who we are, is to a very large extent the result of what we have lived through and experienced, and this extended experience over time is mostly out of our awareness. It could be said it is unconscious, but we find the term unconscious inadequate to describe what we are alluding to. The term implicit memory is a possible way to describe what we are proposing but we find it also a bit misleading because implicit memory is too close to knowledge that we are not consciously accessing. Memory is often defined in one variation or other as basically the faculty by which the mind stores and remembers information. Some have defined it as the faculty or process of retaining information over time, others have defined memory as remembering the past allowing us to find our future path.

What we have in mind, however, with experience, is a lot more than a faculty or a process, it is who we are as a result of what we have experienced from day one, if not from when we were a fetus inside our mothers. This experience is global and events are only a part of it. The baby develops in specific ways based on its interaction with its mother or caretaker, with its father, the environment, its physical health, its hormonal balance, the food it eats, the bed it sleeps in, the way it is held and so on. These experiences from early in life cause us, along with the genetic, epigenetic, endocrine and other contributors, to be who we are. This experience is broader than memory in all its forms. At any single point in our lives we are the resultant of our experiences, and these experiences change and develop over time, with earlier experiences effecting later ones and later ones allowing a re-evaluation of earlier ones but only up to a point. Parenthetically unlike memory, experience is not in the usual course of our life altered or distorted, even though the memory of an experience can be altered or distorted. The above does not imply that memories, especially past memories, as reported in the therapeutic setting are not valuable, but that they are only a small part of the process and as a narrative of the persons life they present guideposts to be deeply explored.

Returning to the question of the therapeutic action of psychoanalysis, the persons who enter psychoanalysis are in addition to the biological, their experiences. What this means is that what they say, how they feel, how they act and react, how they love or hate, how they understand, in sum their thinking, feeling behaving self is based on the experiences of their life. And, this self is affected by new experiences, just as it could be affected by hormonal and other changes. It is this self, in part the sum of experiences, that is the focus of psychoanalytic work. It bears repeating that this view of the mind, namely as the sum of our experiences along with the biological contributions, and the proposal that these experiences create or contribute significantly to creating maps and algorithms that determine our being is at best a simplification given the fact that so much of the workings of the brain and body remain undiscovered.

Another clinical example:

The patient is a young woman who enters analysis at the age of 28. She is dressed in a style that makes her resemble an adolescent boy. Shorts, sneakers and a baseball hat. She is single and has not had any relationship beyond short lasting dates. Men see her more as a friend and one of them rather than an attractive female. She is well educated but has a job just above the lowest level at this firm. She is aware something is wrong. History reveals a cowboy father whom she was very close to and a highly intellectual, cold, distant mother. She has no siblings and maintains a good relationship with her parents who leave far from New York and therefore sees them only on holidays and special family occasions.

Analysis at 5 times a week lasts six years. She moves up to the position of head of department at her firm, marries, has two sons. When she comes to see me years after the end of the analysis she describes herself as satisfied with family and work life. Children older and ready to go off to college, marriage satisfactory, work going very well. She is poised, elegant, self-reflective and very self-possessed. She talks about her analysis, how when in analysis she felt she would just come to her sessions and all problems would be solved, whereas now she has to deal with all the vicissitudes of life. Analysis, she believes. gave her the possibility to navigate life as well as it can be done.

Psychoanalysis itself can be seen as a new, formative experience in a person's life. A successful young man came into treatment because of a persistent but vague feeling of dissatisfaction with himself and with all that he did. He was quite bright, but with a significant, childhood undiagnosed learning disability. His intelligence allowed him to "slip by" in almost all situations, even when he knew he was not doing the work. He would not read the assignment but was able to figure out the right answers. He was charming and manipulative. All of these issues were extensively worked with in a productive, 8 year analysis. He now felt more genuine and deserving of his success.

The patient asked for a follow-up visit about six years post termination. He said that the reason for the visit was to inform the analyst of a significant event that had occurred during the analysis but had never been mentioned. One day the patient paid his bill and instead of writing "Twenty two Hundred and Fifty," he wrote "Twenty Two Fifty." The analyst returned the check and asked that it be rewritten properly. The patient thought to himself, "What an obsessive asshole," but said nothing and brought a new check the next day.

"I soon began mulling over that episode and picking out so many different aspects. My anxiety about saying anything angry to you. Your forthrightness in expressing what you wanted. Your valuing the importance of detail, of getting it right, of reality. My submissiveness. My trying to slide by. My not caring about reality. I know we talked about many of these issues, but this living out of my ways of being next to your ways of being has left a permanent impression on who I am."

The powerful experience of meeting with a new kind of person four or five times a week is what we are focusing on. This new person is interested, curious, non-judgmental, and with no agenda. This experience allows for any and all thoughts to be felt, examined and expressed. An experience like no other experience. And like all previous formative events, relationships and experiences, it is incorporated into the fabric of the analysand's identity. (As well as into the fabric of the analyst.) This may be the most important agent for change. This may be why, when people are asked years later about their analysis, they most often remember events in the analysis rather than insights. "The time my analyst handed back the check I had written because it was not accurate."

In ending, we would say that embarking on a therapeutic journey is like visiting a city (preferring this to the metaphoric description to Freud's train ride) one has visited before but has not delved deep into. Familiarity with the main arteries and sights and a few of the connecting streets has allowed one to navigate and partake in the city life but now the visit is to be for a longer period of time and for the purpose of living in it. More streets will need to be discovered, more sights, more nooks and crannies. Every discovery will facilitate the next discovery and after some time, the visitor now a resident will look back and see how much more he or she knows and how the same destinations can be reached more efficiently, with less worry or anxiety and with an enjoyment heretofore not available or attainable. This is the patient who after a period of time looks back at his or her life and sees how it has been less difficult; not so because life does not have its hardships but easier because the person has not added to those hardships unnecessary complications. The patient who now sees a continuity in her or his life and therefore looks at the future with a certain feeling of empowerment and control.

This increase in knowledge about the city that is our mind is never complete and can never ever be complete during ones life time. Much will remain outside awareness, including sources of anxiety and fear. While an occasional dream may suddenly reveal a hitherto unknown fear, a great deal will always remain out of our reach as therapist and as patient. At the same time, however, with the new and limited knowledge, we would be navigating our world with more ease and hopefully happiness and gratitude.

In ending, we would like to quote from a letter to Stefan Zweig from Freud in October 1937 wherein referring to his work he says: " No one can predict how posterity will assess it. I myself am not completely certain—Doubt can never be divorced from scientific research, and I have surely not discovered more than a small fragment of truth".

The small fragment of truth had and to some degree continues to have a large impact in the way we see the world and ourselves within this world, however, as science has inexorably moved forward, it is time for psychoanalysis to participate in this progress by revisiting its outdated theories.

References

Brenner, C. (2008). Aspects of Psychoanalytic Theory: Drives, defense, and the Pleasure-Unpleasure Principle. *Psychoanalytic Quarterly* 77(3): 707–717.

Freud, S. (1923). The Ego and the Id. *Standard Edition* 19:12–66.

——— (1893–1895). Studies on Hysteria. *Standard Edition* 2:1–305.

——— (1900). Interpretation of Dreams. *Standard Edition* 4, 5.

——— (1905). Three Essays on Sexuality. *Standard Edition* 7:133–243.

——— (1915). The Unconscious. *Standard Edition* 14:159–215.

——— (1926). Inhibitions, Symptoms and Anxiety. *Standard Edition* 20:75–176.

——— (1938). An Outline of Psychoanalysis. *Standard Edition* 23:139–208.

——— (1933). Introductory Lectures on Psychoanalysis. *Standard Edition* 22:89–90.

——— (1920). Beyond the Pleasure Principle. *Standard Edition* 18: 7–64.

———— (1895/1950) Project for a Scientific Psychology. *Standard Edition* 1:283–397.

Inda, M.C., Muravieva, E., & Alberini, C.M. (2011). Memory retrieval and the passage of time: from consolidation and strengthening to extinction. *Journal of Neuroscience* 31:1635–1643.

LeDoux, J. (2012). *Rethinking the Emotional Brain.* 73:653–676. *Neuron.*

Nersessian, E. (2000). A Neuroscientific Perspective on Confabulation: Commentary by Edward Nersessian. *Neuro-Psychoanalysis* 2:163–166.

———— (2011). Conflict Theory. Presented at 100 year anniversary of the New York Psychoanalytic Society.

———— (2013). Psychoanalytic theory of anxiety: proposals for reconsideration, In *On Freud's Inhibitions, Symptoms and Anxiety,* edited by Samuel Arbiser and Jorge Schneider, London: Routledge.

———— (2014). Reassessing Freud's Fundamental Tenets. Presented to the faculty, New York Psychoanalytic Institute.

Panksepp, J. (1998). *Affective Neuroscience: The Foundations of Human and Animal Emotions.* Oxford: Oxford University Press, pp. 191–205.

Stern, P. (2017). Neuroscience: In search of new concepts. *Science* 358(6362): 465–466.

Chapter 6
Why Psychoanalysis Had to Change: Feminism, Relational Theory, and Analyst as a Real Person

Dale S. Gody

Abstract

Criticism around analytic anonymity, neutrality, and abstinence were fundamental to the development of relational theory ushering in the ideas of mutuality, asymmetry, and co-construction. A review of how Freud actually practiced, the historical move from an objectivist position to a constructivist one, and the contributions of feminism shed light on the shifts in technique from a relational perspective. A two-person model of mind and therapeutic action necessitates being real with patients including the necessity of dealing with real events in the patient's experience and the unconscious judgments that impair the analyst's ability to do so. However, technical choices must always assess whether the patient can make use of interpretation or the analyst as a separate subject. While enactment and self-disclosure may be more valued by the relational model than other models, this does not necessitate ignoring the role of the unconscious and the interaction of the intrapsychic with the interpersonal. Increased freedom for the analyst to match needed responses to the patient contributes to the growing capacity for the patient to experience self and other as two subjects as well as intersubjectivity.

Thinking About Psychoanalytic Technique and Shibboleths

Henry Friedman has been a generous and generative thinker about psychoanalysis for many years, writing about the shifts in analytic theory and clinical technique for half a century. In his article he reviews the development of analytic theory and traces the modifications of theory around clinical technique and their implications for the analyst as a person. He demonstrates to us through the change in his own thinking the necessity of the analyst moving from what we might now consider a caricature of psychoanalysis: analytic neutrality, abstinence, and anonymity to a three dimensional, real person who is emotionally engaged with the patient, and emotionally vulnerable in the dyad. Ultimately, he suggests "Once an analyst concludes that the basis for all our theories are indeed theoretical and unable to be either disproven or proven it is possible to face the need to be real with his patients." I heartily agree and want to add some thoughts about how Freud actually practiced, the historical move from an objectivist position to a constructivist one, and the contributions of feminism to shifts in technique from a relational perspective. I hope to also to touch on the necessity of being real with patients including the necessity of dealing with real events in the patient's experience and the unconscious judgments that impair our ability to do so.

The analyst has always been a real person in the analysis, but was constrained early on by a set of rules necessitating a denial of crucial aspects of being a human in some ways that contributed to the evolution of psychoanalysis, but in other ways also stymied analytic freedom and comfort with intimate engagement in important ways. Freud developed his theory with an eye towards garnering acceptance of psycho-analysis as an objective, scientific inquiry.

This necessitated neutrality, abstinence, and anonymity by the analyst as an objective observer. In addition, as Freud (1912a; 1912b; 1915) discovered that transference was a powerful tool in working through the patient's problems, he proposed that these technical stances of the analyst were necessary to facilitate the development of the analyst as a transference object, to help the analyst maintain an objective stance in conflict between id impulses and superego prohibitions, and to facilitate free association, thereby granting access to the unconscious.

While Freud was busy writing about analytic technique and discovering more about how the mind works, he was also seeing patients. Many of these patients traveled from other cities to have their three or four month analyses, dined with Freud, walked with Freud, and even were privy to his own worries. His dogs were included in the consulting room, and his family was in and out of the home, present for meals and at times befriending patients. A review of forty-three cases Freud analyzed found that in all cases Freud deviated from strict anonymity, expressing his own feelings, attitudes, and experiences, including his feelings towards his analysands and his personal worries (Lynn & Valliant, 1998). In other words, despite his written theory about clinical technique, he was often engaged outside of the consulting room as a person, sometimes also as a friend, and sometimes as a teacher. These multiple roles undoubtedly made contributions to the trans-ference and the countertransference. So, on one hand, he thought that maintaining a blank slate was necessary for the transference to develop and for the analyst to maintain sci-entific objectivity, on the other hand he was often quite pres-ent as a subject in his own right. We can assume that it was Freud's followers who enshrined the set of rules regarding neutrality, abstinence, and anonymity since it is clear Freud did not follow his own precepts. Also of interest is Freud's motivation for using the couch. He thought it would induce a relaxed state like hypnosis and facilitate free association, but he also hated to be looked at. "I cannot put up with being stared at by other people for eight hours a day (or more)" (Freud, 1913). So even from the beginning of psychoanalysis with all of Freud's brilliant ideas and objectivist scientific orientation, unquestionably Freud as a person is influencing how his theory develops, and we have inherited, introjected, and idealized these aspects of technique.

Perhaps it is also worth considering that the prospect of emotional intimacy with our patients is both longed for and feared. On the one hand it is enormously gratifying to be invited to explore and engage with the mind and experience of another person, but on the other hand we have all experienced the powerful disruption that such intense involvement can wreak on our own psyches. Thus, for reasons of our own need for self-protection, maintaining anonymity, neutrality, and abstinence can have a certain appeal.

Aron and Starr (2013) in a paper titled "What is Psychoanalysis?" proposed that early on in the history of psychoanalysis three shibboleths emerged to differentiate analytic practitioners as a group from others providing mental health treatment and to create a border or boundary of those who were in the in-group vs. the out-group. These three tenets, well known to all of us in the in-group include 1) the role of the unconscious, 2) the use of dream or depth theory, 3) the centrality of the Oedipus complex. Later when psychoanalysis came to the United States, a further effort to maintain the in-group of the privileged and a monopoly on psychoanalysis necessitated excluding lay practitioners and requiring medical degrees of those who could be admitted to this exclusive club. These limitations only came to an end in 1998 after a class action suit brought by psychologists against the American Psychoanalytic Association. My point here is to highlight that some of the original rules about technique were not only to establish psychoanalysis as a science and to facilitate analytic process, but ultimately protect the analyst from too many disruptive feelings, and to maintain privilege by limiting membership to those who agreed to practice according to a strict set of rules.

The opening up of this exclusive club coincided with a move away from an objectivist philosophy and the view that the analyst because of his privileged position of knowing more about the patient and being healthier than the patient, could rely on his own observations to be unimpeded by himself. Postmodern theory challenged assumptions of analytic neutrality, objectivity, and certainty from an epistemological position. How do we know what we know?

Of significant import, feminist theory and infant observation had been percolating and raising questions about the accepted binary around gender, the role of power relations, and view of the mother as only an object in the mind of the infant. Briefly, the first feminist critiques challenged the classical model of development as an androcentric model: the normal human is male, the female is defective. Feminist critics highlighted the idea that this view represented a little boy's view on sexuality, overlooked female experience of sexuality, neglected the power differential of men and women in society, thus perpetuated patriarchy (Horney, 1924; Thompson, 1953). The second wave of feminism focused on gender difference and critiqued the view of autonomy as the hallmark of emotional maturity. This critique also framed the value of relationship and caring as a separate but equal province of women, unfortunately maintaining and reifying the binary (Dimen, 2013). Fortunately, a third wave of feminism emerged. Gender feminism began with the position that the subjectivity of the mother is unacknowledged by culture (Benjamin,1998). Instead, the mother is viewed as an object in the world of the child and the greater world, not an autonomous subject who is essential in helping the child develop. Over time, the importance of the mother as a subject emerged, supported by the work of infant observation. Infant researchers like Beatrice Beebe and Frank Lachman (1998), Daniel Stern (1985), and later attachment theorists noted the reciprocal interaction between mother (main caregiver)

111

and infant. Mothers provide acknowledgement of the baby as a subject, suspending their own needs in order to respond to those of the child. Their ability to do so contributes to the child's capacity to experience the mother as a subject, and to the capacity for mutuality. The recognition of maternal subjectivity and bidirectional interaction with baby initiating and seeking relationship propelled the relational movement in psychoanalysis to move from a one-person model to a two-person model of mind in analytic process. This third step of feminism pressed for a move from dualism to multiplicity, embracing the constructivist position. As a post-modern theory it abandons the belief in an essential, unique, individual identity instead viewing internal life as an historical production, a creation that emerges in a field of power relations and with no set paths around gender and sexuality (Chodorow, 1992). Human subjectivity is viewed as contingent upon and constituted culturally and politically through language. The internal world influences the external world, the external world influences the internal world. Intrapsychic functioning influences interpersonal relations, and interpersonal experience influences intrapsychic functioning. Meaning is individually constructed and highly influenced by fantasy. From my vantage point feminism was necessary to usher in the possibility of the analyst functioning as a real subject, not only an object in the analytic dyad.

Relational theory maintains that experience is inherently ambiguous and that the analyst as well as the patient is motivated by unconscious processes so that we can never really fully know our own minds nor those of our patients (Davies, 2018). While relational theorists often lean on other theories such as object relations or self-psychology, central to relational theory is the idea that the analyst's subjectivity is always present and influences what happens in the consulting room, whether we want to acknowledge that or not. Furthermore, it suggests that there is mutual and bi-directional influence, both conscious and unconscious, between analyst and patient which contributes to the analytic process in the dyad (Aron, 1991). There are two minds in the consulting room, both conscious and unconscious, even if one of them cannot always acknowledge the presence of the other separate mind. Many years ago, Lucia Tower (1956) suggested that there is unconscious to unconscious communication between the analytic pair, an idea that seemed radical at the time but has been embraced by many clinicians today. In fact, in this paper she reports challenging her analytic supervisee who was struggling with his erotic fantasies to his patient with the quip, "How do you know that telling her about them might not be helpful to her?"

Necessary Shifts in Clinical Technique and Therapeutic Action

The de-idealization of the analyst's authority, the ambiguity of experience, the uncertainty of knowing self and other makes the reconstruction of history an impossibility and an unproductive analytic pursuit. More accessible and useful is a focus on the patient's experience of self, other, and self in relation to other, both conscious and unconscious. And concomitantly, an exploration by the analyst of her own experience, both conscious and unconscious of self, other, and self in relation to the patient in the here and now. Admittedly this is a big demand. Merton Gill, a Chicago psychoanalyst with whom I studied before entering my analytic training, always emphasized the piece of reality in each moment of transference and how the exploration of this in the 'here and now' would generally lead to the 'there and then'. A focus on transference and countertransference remains central to relational psychoanalysis, with room to explore both genetic contributions, the role of fantasy, and the real relationship between the patient and analyst (Gill, 1983).

Moving from a reliance upon free association and interpretation, which is not possible with any number of patients, to consideration about what is happening in the room between patient and analyst, relational theorists seek to make use of our own immediate experience of the patient in the context of the patient's history, experience of self/selves, other, and interpersonal schemas. Of course, all of these elements are also present in the room for the analyst as well. Ehrenberg (2010) highlighted this as "the intimate edge" noting that there is no real treatment unless the analyst makes herself emotionally vulnerable and engages in the patient's emotional world. Kleinian theory highlights the role of affect as unformulated experience that begins with bodily sensation which can become thought when held and contained by the analyst and then symbolized in language (Klein, 1923). One of the ways relational theorists engage with patients is by tuning in to their own bodily experience and reverie with the assumption that they are resonating with aspects of the patient or their own experience and that an exploration of this with the patient is likely to lead to more clarity. With the idea in mind that we cannot know our own unconscious, relational clinicians extend an invitation to the patient to consider what the analyst might be experiencing to contribute to the co-creation of meaning. Critics have suggested that relational theorists are overly focused on, and promote, enactments in order to facilitate exploration and growth. In my opinion this is a mischaracterization of the relational frame. Enactments are prevalent in big and small ways from the beginning of most analytic treatments and the ability of the analyst to take a step backwards to consider her own contribution to these seems essential in order for both patient and analyst to understand what is happening between them. The choice for the analyst is whether to, when to, and how to disclose aspects of the analyst's experience that have contributed to the enactment. Sometimes the analyst has been on the receiving end of a projective identification and must work her way around to see what she has been holding or identifying with that belongs to the patient or the patient's objects. And sometimes the analyst must confront her own conflicts, limitations, and internalized objects that have become mobilized. And most of the time both of these things are true at the same time, sometimes creating a fiery sexy tango and sometimes creating an icy death spiral. In the exploration of what just happened here, the analyst's subjectivity is almost always in the spotlight, under scrutiny by the patient, like it or not.

This highlights another important aspect to the analyst's presence as a person being an essential and inescapable participant in the process. Instead of assuming an objective and neutral position, the analyst is always revealed in one way or another as a vulnerable human being. There was more protection around this when the analyst could function as a mainly detached authority and maintain allegiance to the set of rules around anonymity, neutrality and abstinence. But increasingly, we are pressed, pulled, or even consciously choose to reveal ourselves as vulnerable people who, like the patient, can be hurt, angry, sad, disappointed, envious, etc. Instead of this necessarily derailing the transference and the possibility of insight, our patients have the possibility of finding a new object, and a separate subject, one who is open to looking at herself, curious about the patient's experience, and one's own, and a model of how to contain one's own emotional response while holding the other in mind. The efforts of the analyst to understand the patient at a deep level and to explore the multiple possible meanings of what has happened between patient and analyst becomes a central avenue of therapeutic action. In this manner the analyst provides recognition of the patient's experience and facilitates self-reflection for the patient. And hopefully having engaged in thinking about what just happened with the patient, including the unconscious contributions from the analyst, the patient will develop more capacity for recognizing the analyst as a separate subject, as well as develop more capacity for recognizing intersubjective experience.

I think it is fair to say wherever your theoretical inclinations lean, we can agree that there is no longer any one model of psychoanalysis that fits all analysts or is usable by all patients, and that we have generally moved in the direction that the analyst is not and cannot be the arbiter of the patient's reality, or for that matter, of her own experience. Most modern theory seems to embrace the view that the subjectivity of the analyst influences the choices that the analyst makes in terms of interventions, and that it is not possible to check either our theory or our unconscious at the door to the consulting room. Each major analytic theory has highlighted this from a particular vantage point. Modern classical theory while still focused on "an attempt to build complex preconscious representations from simple unconscious representations and presentations…has expanded to incorporate greater attunement to and use of countertransference reactions, understanding the importance of analysts empathic attunement, the role of analyst as co-contributor to the analysis" (Busch, 2023). Irma Brenman Pick (2018) highlights the view from object relations theory that close attention to the countertransference and the analyst's working through of it enables the analyst to experience the patient's inner world, digest it, formulate it, and interpret with authenticity. Self-psychology moved from the view of optimal frustration as the cornerstone of therapeutic action to the view that optimal responsiveness of the analyst is curative (Bacal, 1985). And more recently, Steve Stern (2017) with a self-psychological relational bent has proposed that progressive fittedness between analyst and patient enables the co-created conditions that facilitate the conditions for the patient's growth. He also highlights the necessary improvisational freedom of the analyst to find this path.

Another factor pressing the analyst to make use of herself as a subject relates to major cultural shifts in our world. Increasingly we are confronted with the reality that external events such as ongoing racism or white privilege, class differences, fluidity of gender and sexuality, culture, religion, climate change, and increasing political hostility and divisions are imbricated in psychic and interpersonal life. Alive and well (not always so well) in the consulting room. The real world influences the internal world. Thus, it is inevitable that the real world experiences of the analyst make their imprint on both conscious attitudes and unconscious experience, just as they do on our patients. We must acknowledge the ways these factors become imbricated in analytic practice and the analytic relationship. Our patients rightly feel pressed to tell us that we do not and perhaps cannot really understand their experiences of discrimination, being othered, alienated, assaulted, silenced, judged from our positions of privilege. And we are forced to turn the eye on ourselves and to acknowledge painful aspects of our patient's and our own unconscious, their mutual influence and the impact of realities on intrapsychic and interpersonal functioning. In this model the "goals of psychoanalysis become authenticity, freedom of expression, expanded relatedness rather than acquisition of insight, although insight is still important it is not privileged over these goals" (Stern, 1988).

"Being real isn't how you are made, it's a thing that happens to you."

This quote from *The Velveteen Rabbit* (Williams, 1922) highlights for me a fundamental truth: we come into the world as infants and while we are real biological beings, we need the recognition of the other to develop a mind, and relational theory suggests for the baby to develop the capacity to acknowledge two minds and the possibility of intersubjectivity. This recognition includes having a parent who can attend to our emotional states by imagining their way into our experience and by responding with emotional regulation, containing, and trying to ascertain what we need as infants. In this manner the parent is able to transform raw affect into thought, such as, "Oh, you must be hungry! Let me sit down to nurse you." Friedman (2023) highlights that what analysands recall as most important during analysis were "the small moments of unexpected human exchange with the analyst." In other words, it was not a genetic, defense, or transference interpretation, but when the analyst intuited what the patient needed and responded in a way that conveyed recognition and caring, and perhaps an openness to engage emotionally. In an earlier paper, Friedman (2020) suggested that it is the relational depth, "one that senses the mutuality between analyst and patient, the caring, the responsiveness, the presence of each other's minds and emotions that results in interpretations not of drive derivatives but of life experiences and the dynamics of relating."

Increasingly we are seeing patients who cannot make use of interpretation, whose early trauma and developmental experiences make them very vulnerable to experiencing interpretation as an assault or a criticism. Even though we try to make assessments of analyzability and capacity for self-reflection at the start of analysis, we can only learn by trial and error what each patient can and cannot use and how we need to be real to facilitate each patient's growth. To be real, and sometimes to become real and usable for the patient, we must, like the parent, rely on some aspect of our emotional resonance or identification with them to discover and recognize what they need. This does not necessitate self-disclosures of our own conflicts and traumas, as many critics of relational theory have imagined, but an openness to considering how we are contributing unconsciously and consciously to the analytic process that evolves with our patients, and remaining open to learning from the patient what they might see about us that has been unconscious for us.

I worked with a middle aged woman who functioned very well at work, but who had great difficulties sustaining intimacy with her partner. She reported that her friends could not believe that she, of all people, needed analysis since they thought she was the most together person they knew. During the first six months of analysis, I made a number of transference interpretations based upon derivative material to which she would exclaim, "What are you talking about? I was telling you about my interaction with my friend. This has nothing to do with you!" Only after several such interactions and a consultation was I able to understand that she did not experience me as a separate person, but needed me as a self-object. When I moved to a mainly empathic and exploratory stance and began to name feelings she did not know she had, our work progressed. Considerable material emerged about her role as her mother's confidante, her father's need for her to achieve success and status in his occupation, and the relative lack of parental interest in the patient's inner life. Through more affirmative interventions such as, "It's understandable that you try so hard to please me and worry about whether you are a good patient, given how much you had to take care of both your mother and father," she was able to look more at her conflict between asserting her own needs, and fears that to assert them in her relationship would result in rejection and abandonment. Throughout much of the analysis I was idealized or experienced as a twin. The patient offered me small gifts such as homemade cookies at holidays, flower bouquets from her garden. Because I did not see these actions as interfering in our work, or as defensive efforts around aggression or erotic overtures, I accepted these gifts without interpretation or exploration. I understood they represented both her appreciation of our work, our real relationship, and her tendency towards accommodation. Over time we were able to talk about how much she wanted my approval and love and how this replicated her relationship with her mother and contributed to her denial of her own needs and feelings in favor of accommodation. Aspects of negative transference later emerged, but mainly in a derivative manner. At times, she complained that the plants in my waiting room appeared neglected, that one even had a hole in the leaf with a sharp sticker punched through it. These observations were easier for her to explore than her more immediate reactions to our interpersonal interaction. It seemed clear that her comments about the plants were related to transference concerns about whether I could be consistently attentive to her needs as well as her fears that I might hurt her not only by neglecting to care for her, but by being too aggressively probing her inner life. My approach to these events was not much different from what I think most analysts might take, that is to explore her fantasies about me as caretaker of the plants and her psyche, to consider what was happening between us that might have felt neglectful or dangerous. A more classical position might have addressed her defensive avoidance of her aggression or mine, of her tendency to accommodate rather than to assert herself. But for a good part of the analysis, she needed me to be more of a container or a self-object and the injection of my own ideas about her would have been experienced as empathic ruptures. I thought that most of the time she needed me to help her understand and to validate her experience, to help her identify her emotions, and to better regulate her states of tension. These seemed like essential building blocks to help her grow in her capacity to find a more authentic self, and to be able to engage with another person with more freedom, including moving to a recognition that each person was a separate subject with their own feelings, thoughts, and needs, and the capacity to find joy in the creation of intersubjective experience.

Much later, towards the end of her analysis, when she referred to me by my husband's last name, one I had never adopted, I bristled, saying "I don't think I have ever used my husband's name." Feeling temporarily unrecognized and perhaps diminished too as the separate person I wanted to claim in retaining my own name. In an effort to own my real experience I disclosed, "I guess you hit a sore spot with me." I shared that it had always been important to me to retain my own name and independence and asked her how she experienced my petulant reaction. She was able to express her recognition of the importance of this to me, and to comment that we had elected different paths in terms of choosing or rejecting our partner's last names. I thought this was an important step for her to acknowledge that we were different and we had made different choices, and commented that she was correct about having touched a nerve in me. Over time I noted her growing ability to make space for me as a separate subject who could offer an idea about her conflicts that she could not see, and her increasing curiosity about me, signs that now there could be two people in the room, not just one. But first as Slavin and Kriegman (1998) highlighted, the therapist had to change! During the termination phase my patient shared, "I love you. You have been such a help to me." With no hesitation, I shared, "I love you too and I am so happy to see how much you have gained from our work together." Two people in a real relationship, speaking their truths to each other.

With another analysand, our treatment began with a series of efforts by the patient to set the fee and the times of the sessions. This patient presented a paucity of material, frequently remaining silent and rejecting most explorations I attempted about the meaning of the silence and the efforts to set the frame. As you might imagine, this was a rather challenging way to start. I knew that in a previous analytic endeavor, the analysis ended when the analyst interpreted these issues as resistance, and ultimately the analyst refused to continue the work.

In the first year there were multiple disruptions: arriving late for appointments, disrupting sessions to take phone calls, to speak with others in the home. For the treatment to go forward I had to find a way to listen to him, to manage my own feelings of frustration and helplessness, to contain both my own disruption and the patient's fear of opening up in the treatment. In a reverie during the patient's silence one day, I recalled my own feelings of helplessness around caring for my premature daughter who was colicky for seven months, and the pain of not being able to soothe her except by nursing. I was too young or too immature to appreciate that being able to tolerate her dysregulated states was what she needed, an acceptance of all of her emotional states without me believing I could always make her happy. Musing about this enabled me to work at staying emotionally present in these silent times. Staying real with him became much easier as the picture of a young boy abandoned by his father, and controlled by a critical, dominating mother, very slowly began to emerge. In other words, wrestling with my own sense of vulnerability and helplessness enabled me to help him to get in touch with his enormous vulnerability and to remain in an empathic state, at least more of the time. Sometimes we have to remind ourselves that holding, containing, managing tension states, is an essential part of treatment and represents not just a technical activity but is fundamentally a needed human response.

About a year into this analysis there were two enactments that proved to be generative. The day before the first occurred I had informed the patient of several upcoming sessions I needed to cancel. At the time he did not share any reaction, nor did I hear any derivative communication about it. But during our next online session the patient received a text and asked me if it was okay to answer it. I wondered with the patient about both his question and the urgency of the text. The patient explained that he had earlier sent a text asking someone to help repair his computer and he didn't want to make this person wait, adding that he hates to wait. In an effort to grant the patient some autonomy I told the patient it was his decision what to do. The patient chose to temporarily shut off the video and audio on Zoom to send the text. I was aware of feeling irritated as there had been many such intrusions in the analytic hours: food deliveries, time out for conversations with the roommate, arriving late to appointments due to poor planning, and also as mentioned above, a resistance to engage by remaining silent and rejecting explorations of these events. But most of this was not really in my awareness when I said to the patient, "I'm wondering what felt so urgent for you to choose disrupting our session to return that text?"

My patient told me that he thought he had asked for permission and that I had left it up to him so he didn't understand why I seemed to be irritated or even mad that he had chosen to do so. I asked the patient what he might imagine I was experiencing, but this was not productive, and as often happens we were at the end of the session and could not process it further that day.

I went to bed ruminating about what had happened and my sleep was very disrupted. I knew that I was feeling anxious, particularly disturbed. When I woke up I remembered that I had a dream about the patient, but the only thing I could remember was this sentence, "For a change, I was able to be patient." My first thought was that this was a self-rep-rimand; you should be more patient. Then I wondered if I felt myself in this interaction to be the patient, the one who like the actual patient could not wait, and who felt frustrated and abandoned too frequently in the analysis, a concordant identification. Next I asked myself, aside from what you know about yourself in these regards, what had happened recently in the analysis that might have contributed to this unconscious enactment in which I gave the patient the space to choose what to do, and then criticized him for doing so. I considered that I was conflicted between wanting to give the patient autonomy in making the decision and wanting the patient to remain emotionally engaged in our analytic rela-tionship. I thought about whether I was on the receiving end of a projective identification in which the patient was uncon-sciously asking me to hold his impatience and or abandon-ment or if I was in this moment in the position of his critical and controlling mother. Maybe any or all of these things. But what to do about all of this?

The patient made no reference to this enactment snafu at the beginning of the session but remained tight lipped and dis-engaged. After waiting five or so minutes to see what might emerge, I suggested that it seemed like there was an elephant in the room related to the last session and I hoped we could explore it together. The patient initially stated that he had already said what he had to say about it yesterday. I nudged him a bit saying, "I'm wondering how you felt about my irri-tation regarding the texting and what you made of it?" My patient responded by saying that it was important to him to have my approval that he was a good patient and he hoped I could understand that he just really needed to respond to that text. He was worried that I was angry at him. I shared that I was more irritated and frustrated about the disruption than angry, as it seemed to be a more frequent occurrence than was optimal for our work. I offered that it seemed the patient was in conflict, one part of him wanted the analysis, the help it might offer, and my approval, and another part of him seemed to absent himself from the analysis through frequent silence, disruptions in the hour, etc. In what may have been a second enactment, I stated that part of my frustration was that I wanted to get to know more about his experience and to better understand him and it seemed that this was scary to him. Since these interventions had not been well received previously I was very surprised when my analysand offered that he thought I was right about that; in fact, it was very scary to open up for fear of criticism, attack, and abandonment. I was able to frame this experience not only to what had just happened in our interaction but also to the previous failed analysis, and early experiences with his controlling mother and abandoning father. Then I wondered out loud if my having shared the day before the snafu that I would be missing a few sessions in the upcoming two weeks had something to do with the patient absenting himself from our work to return the text. The patient again surprisingly considered that perhaps as much as he enjoyed saving the fee during my absence, he did feel abandoned, so he might have wanted to leave me because he was angry that I could just leave when I wanted to. "Why might I want to leave you?" I asked. "Maybe because I am after all not such a good patient." he responded. I felt a door was opening in our work to consider more about the patient's resistance as an effort not only to be in control but also to protect himself from his conflict around the wish for closeness and fear of it, and his fears about his own aggression. Being real with him about my irritation, and my wish to know him at a deeper level seemed crucial to this shift. The two enactments, the first one of my unconscious criticism about his returning the text, and the second of my effort to engage with him emotionally, proved generative.

In closing, I hope psychoanalysis will continue to evolve and that we can make space for using a variety of theories of therapeutic action since no one theory is useful for every analytic dyad. Fred Busch (2023) likens this view to a psychoanalytic forest where the resources flow from the oldest and biggest trees (classical theory) to the youngest and smallest (later theoretical models), but I think it also worth considering that all trees must make adaptations over time in order to survive. New ways of thinking about analytic theory and clinical process are always emerging and enriching the core of psychoanalysis. The realities of our cultural diversity, gender and sexuality diversity, political conflicts, and crises and traumas will also impact the directions that theories and techniques evolve. Our job as teachers, supervisors, and clinicians is to champion the analytic inquiry, not to hold tight to ideas about the right way to do analysis. It is no longer possible or desirable to hide behind theory and a set of arbitrary rules which tend to dehumanize the analytic relationship rather than reinvigorate the joy of emotional engagement and facilitate the depth of psychic exploration.

References

Aron, L. (1991). The Patient's Experience of the Analyst's Subjectivity. *Psychoanalytic Dialogues,* 1:29–51.

——— & Starr, K. (2013). What is Psychoanalysis? Can You Say "Shibboleth?" In *Psychotherapy for the People,* Chapter 17, 357–379.

Bacal, H.A. (1985). Optimal Responsiveness and the Therapeutic Process. *Progress in Self Psychology,* 1:202–227.

Beebe, B. & Lachmann, F.M. (1998). Co-constructing Inner and Relational Processes: Self and Mutual Regulation in Infant Research and Adult treatment. *Psychoanalytic Psychology,* 15:480–516.

Benjamin, J. (1998). *Shadow of the Other.* London and New York: Routledge.

Brenman Pick, I. (2018). *Authenticity in the Psychoanalytic Encounter.* London and New York: Routledge.

Busch, F. (2023). How to Grow a Psychoanalytic Forest, Chapter 5 in *Psychoanalysis at the Crossroads,* 74–86. London and New York: Routledge.

Chodorow, N.J. (1992). Heterosexuality as a Compromise Formation. *Psychoanalysis. Contemporary Thought,* 15(3):267–304.

Davies, J.M. (2018). The "Rituals of Relational Perspective: Theoretical Shifts and Clinical Implications. *Psychoanalytic Dialogues,* 28:651–669.

Dimen, M. (2013). The Third Step: Freud, the Feminists, and Postmodernism. Chapter 2 In *Sexuality, Intimacy, and Power,* pp. 63–81.

Ehrenberg, D. (2010). Working at the Intimate Edge. *Contemporary Psychoanalysis,* 46:120–141.

Freud, S. (1912a). The Dynamics of Transference. *Standard Edition,* 12:227–238.

——— (1912b). Recommendations to Physicians Practicing Psycho-analysis. *Standard Edition,* 12:109–120.

——— (1913). On Beginning the Treatment (Further Recommendations on the Technique of Psycho-Analysis. *Standard Edition,* 12:121–144.

——— (1915). Observations on Transference Love (Further Recommendations on the Technique of Psycho-Analysis III). *Standard Edition,* 12:157–171.

Friedman, H.J. (2022). The Need for and Resistance to Realness in the Analyst: Making Psychoanalysis a Truly Two-Person Experience. *Psychoanalytic Inquiry,* 40:262–270.

——— (2023). The Problem of Psychoanalytic Anonymity: The Obstacles Created by the Persistence of Traditional Technique. *International Journal of Controversial Discussions,* this volume, p. 3–22.

Gill, M. (1983). *The Analysis of the Transference Theory and Technique.* Madison, CT: International Universities Press.

Horney, K. (1926). On the Genesis of Castration Anxiety. *International Journal of Psychoanalysis*, 5:50–65.

Klein, M. (1923). The Development of a Child. *International Journal of Psycho-Analysis*, 4:419–474.

Lynn, D. & Valliant, G. (1998). Anonymity, Neutrality, and Confidentiality in the Actual Methods of Sigmund Freud: A Review of Forty Three Cases, 1907–1939. *American Journal of Psychiatry*, 155(2):163–171.

Miller, M. (1922). *The Velveteen Rabbit*. Doubleday Books, 1991.

Slavin, M.O. & Kriegman, D. (1998). Why the Analyst Has to Change: Toward a Theory of Conflict, Negotiation, and Mutual Influence in the Therapeutic Process. *Psychoanalytic Dialogues* 8:247–284.

Stern, D. (1985). *The Interpersonal World of the Infant*. New York: Basic Books.

———— (1988). The Eye Sees Itself. In Wolstein, B. ed, *Essential Papers on Countertransference*. New York: New York University Press, pp. 229–253.

Stern, S. (2017). Understanding and Engagement in the Analytic Process, In *Needed Relationships and Psychoanalytic Healing: A Holistic Relational Perspective on the Therapeutic Process*. London and New York: Routledge, pp. 109–150.

Thompson, C. (1953). Psychology of Women. *Pastoral Psychology*, 4(34):29–38.

Tower, L. (1956). Countertransference. *Journal of the American Psychoanalytic Association*, 4:224–255.

Chapter 7
The Analyst's Personality as an
Element of Psychoanalytic Technique

Neal Spira

Intro

It may seem obvious that what we do as analysts has a lot to do with who we are as people as well as what we do as interpreters of our patients' subjective experience. Yet when it comes to the teaching of analytic technique, our literature has not offered much guidance on how to use our unique personalities as "analytic instruments," despite our appreciation that the analyst is, unavoidably, a direct participant in the construction of the analytic experience. This evolution of perspective on the nature of what we do would seem to call for a revisiting of our ideas about what constitutes analytic technique and how to teach it. The following paper is a beginning effort.

I. Freud

Any discussion of psychoanalytic technique needs to give its due to Freud's original efforts to set down on paper what he actually did with patients. The 5 papers he devoted to this topic (Freud, 1912, 1913, 1914, 1915) were the accumulated wisdom of years of clinical experience with a method that was largely the product of his own creative genius. Yet Freud's own forceful personality probably played as large a role as his genius in all of the endeavors that put psychoanalysis on the map, including his clinical work. He was bold. His own boldness in developing "the analytic situation" allowed him to have the experiences that informed his theorizing about the nature of the mind. And in reciprocal manner, setting the stage for future psychoanalytic generations, his theory informed his technique. Thus, his recommendation that analysis was best done with an attitude of abstinence derived from "Topographic concepts" that he had thus far found most useful in organizing the data that he had obtained clinically. This recommendation suggested that the analyst's personality was something to be, for the most part, suppressed—as if this were possible for a man like Freud, let alone the rest of us.

Freud realized that the technical procedures he endorsed were particularly suited to his own personality, and he said as much (Freud, 1912, p. 111), calling them "recommendations." Perhaps his recognition of his own forcefulness inclined him toward an emphasis on restraint in accordance with the theory he had developed at that point in his career, a theory in which he clearly had a great personal investment. At the same time, what Freud actually DID with his patients seems to have been a reflection of a personality that was anything but restrained. As Lipton (1977) and others have pointed out, Freud seemed to take for granted that the analytic procedure would be superimposed on a REAL RELATIONSHIP in which the analyst's personality found ample room for expression. This relationship, with all of it's suggestive elements, resided somewhere outside the realm of technique until it was placed center stage by Franz Alexander and Thomas French, with their controversial concept of "The Corrective Emotional Experience."

II. The Corrective Emotional Experience

The essence of the CEE was the recommendation analysts depart from analytic abstinence and use their own personality characteristics in a manner that might be particularly suited to the needs of each particular patient. (This orientation, if not explicitly stated, had been implied by their analytic predecessors Ferenczi and Rank as early as 1925.) Alexander based this recommendation on his interpretation of classical "structural" psychoanalytic theory, which rooted psychopathology in maladaptive defense mechanisms that had been, at least in part, an ineffective response to a pathogenic emotional environment.

Alexander's work evoked a strong negative reaction among his peers, locally and nationally. He is commonly caricatured as encouraging analysts to present themselves in a fraudulent way by playing a role that was not authentic to them. But looking back on his work, it appears that he was trying to open things up by allowing analysts to use those aspects of their personalities that were authentic, as opposed to hiding them behind the artificial posture of detachment. As summarized by Bacal (1990) Alexander buttressed his thesis by drawing attention to the fact that the usual analytic attitude of objective detachment "is itself an adopted and studied attitude and not a spontaneous reaction to the patient" (p. 94). He made it quite clear that he was not advocating that the analyst attempt to hide the true nature of his personality from the patient or to play the role of a significant figure of his past in a better way. He was, rather, recommending that the analyst deliberately plan to modify his attitudes according to his understanding of the patient's original conflict situation, in order both to reactivate the patient's early attitudes and to create an interpersonal atmosphere that will provide the patient with emotional experiences in his relationship with the therapist that would "correct," or alter, reaction patterns that are currently maladaptive (see Alexander & French, 1946, p. 76 and Alexander, 1956, pp. 101–102).

131

In addition to the accusation of inauthenticity was the criticism that Alexander was advocating an overtly suggestive technique and calling it "psychoanalysis," a brand that defined itself by it's distance from suggestion and it's proximity to more objective "truth" residing inside the patient and independent of the analyst, whose function was not to influence, but to interpret.

Kurt Eissler (1953) was particularly influential in establishing an equivalence between analytic technique and interpretation, making the case—based on his own interpretation of theory—that the analyst's personality and the patient's particular life circumstances were extraneous factors that, while meriting consideration, were not, fundamentally, relevant to what was psychoanalytic in psychoanalytic technique.

III. The Swing of the Pendulum

As we know, the pendulum has swung far in the other direction. Preceded by Winnicott's work on "the facilitating environment" and Balint's attempts to direct our attention to developmental needs instead of unconscious wishes, Kohut's self psychology led to a new emphasis on the analyst's responsiveness as central to the technique of analyzing. An increasing comfort with discussing countertransference has led to greater clarity in recognizing that the analyst's responses were not always (or seldom) consciously constructed. In other words, as a analyst, no matter how much you try to "sit out", you can't help but play or expend energy trying to convince yourself and, possibly, your patient, that you are not a player.

While this pendulum swing, like it's countermovement, is rationalized on epistemologic and theoretical considerations (a reaction to positivism, post-modern perspectival thinking, intersubjective theory), the fact remains that it has proved impossible to keep the analyst's personality out of the room. Our multiplicity of contemporary psychoanalytic "theories" appear to find common ground in the space they provide for the emergence of the analyst's personality. Perhaps the very fact of our theoretical pluralism provides a kind of testimony to the irrepressible way in which our personalities find expression in the theories we create to solve the dilemma of what to do with our personalities.

Of particular note is the ascendancy of the interpersonal theory of "Enactments" within the psychoanalytic mainstream (Boston Change Group Panel Report, *JAPA* 2013) (and, lagging far behind, the eventual incorporation of the WAW Institute into the American Psychoanalytic Association). The idea that patient and analyst are inevitably destined to react to one another according to the dictates of their unconscious, and that useful meaning can be derived from this interplay has come along with a greater readiness to play on the part of the analyst, whose non-interpretive (and often non-verbal!) responses are now well within the scope of technique.

IV. Intertwining Modalities of Psychoanalytic Technique

To the extent that analytic technique is a function of the totality of the analyst's responses, a conversation about analytic technique should include a discussion about the analyst's use of his own personality, and his relationship and attitude toward his own responses—conscious and otherwise.

I think that efforts in this direction can be facilitated by the recognition that there are, in fact, two modalities of technique, each necessary but not sufficient to support a psychoanalytic treatment. One is the hermeneutic modality, the modality of interpretation. The other—whether we call it suggestion, provision, parameter, optimal responsiveness, or a corrective emotional experience—has to do with the use of the analyst's unique personality. In the dialectic unfolding of these two aspects of psychoanalytic intervention over our history, they have often appeared as antithetical, while in fact the one is inseparable from the other.

The pursuit of meanings can become a meaningless intellectual exercise if not accompanied by a compelling experience (as Ferenzci, Rank, and Alexander suggested). The pursuit of "connection" can lead away from the reflective distance needed to raise the question "what does this all mean?"

Thus, we may think of necessary and sufficient conditions for analysis. Neither the search for meaning or the striving for relationship is sufficient for generating a fruitful psychoanalytic situation, and the two are both essential ingredients of psychoanalytic technique.

V. New Recommendations for Clinicians Practicing PSA

Our discussion of technique is particularly relevant to the field of psychoanalytic education. The "Eitington" educational model which we follow in the United States involves 3 elements—the analyst's analysis, supervision and didactic. Analysis and supervision provide the experiential basis for learning that carry the most weight in the analytic educational process. But in addition to such experience, as stewards of analytic education we should strive to provide our students with a cohesive and contemporary set of principles appropriate to the experience of the analyst who is sitting, listening, thinking, and, at a conscious level, making decisions about what to say.

It seems to me that the best organizing principles here are to think of technique in terms of the cultivation of ATTITUDES. Freud himself suggested this in discussing the "attitude of interest" that was useful in attaching the patient to the analyst—a small throwaway sentence of huge importance (Freud, 1913, p. 139). Years later, Roy Schafer (1983) used this organizing principle to encompass a spectrum of relational and interpretive functions. Schafer was prescient in anticipating the continued shifting sands that would require a new way of thinking about how to keep one's bearings— back in the 1980's, at a time when postmodern sensibilities were starting to take hold.

Schafer recommended that the analyst SUBORDINATE his/her personality in the service of the analytic task—recognizing that it could not be eliminated. He elaborated on this by introducing the idea of the analysts "second self," characterized by attitude of neutrality, empathy, affirmation and the privileging of interpretation. (Schafer saw this as the counterpart to a "second self" that the analysand brings to the consulting room. The analyst's second self is the analyst at his best, in contrast to the analysand's, which is often the patient at his worst.)

But, as I am asserting here, despite our best efforts at "subordination," the analyst's "working ego" or second self is inseparable from those elements of the analyst's personality that inevitably accompany the analyst from one side of the consulting room door to the other. One impact of relational thinking and the general acceptance of "enactments" as a legitimate locus for therapeutic action is that over the last several years we analysts have allowed ourselves to become increasingly entangled in the therapeutic process, and that much more free to be ourselves, in ways that reflect our uniqueness as well as the "analytic ideal" that we strive to achieve. This puts our own knowledge of who were are and how we effect others right up front as something we need to consider. Thus, some additional recommendations may be in order.

The first recommendation goes like this:

1. Be open to learn about yourself from your patients.

In addition to one's own analysis, we can learn a tremendous amount about ourselves from our significant others—those patients who allow us to get to know them over time. They get to know us as well, if we let them. While as analysts we are trained to look at the transference aspects of our patient's communications to us, they provide us with even more information about the non-transference aspects of how we impact on them. (Irwin Hoffman, following Merton Gill, has been pivotal in raising the curtain on this aspect of our work.)

135

This information is important because it can guide us in discerning what we do that is helpful and what we do that is not as we strive to use the best of who we are to relate (one essential element of technique) in a manner that will permit us to interpret (the other essential element). But our ability to usefully access and employ this information is limited by the degree to which the perceptions of our patients pose a threat to our psychological equilibrium.

The recognition that we might be as visible to our patients as they are to us can be unnerving. Patients are, inevitably, a source of our self esteem to the extent that they provide us the privilege of allowing us to be their analysts. But the opposite is also true: Patients can hurt our feelings. When they tell us something about ourselves that we might not want to know, it can be just as painful as when we tell patients something about themselves that they would rather not know. This is a threat that can't be eliminated simply by putting them on a couch so they can't see us, or by attributing all that they see to the perceptual distortions of transference.

Freud engaged this difficulty by recommending that the analyst needs an analysis. Our educational tradition has wisely incorporated the personal analysis as the way in which we as analysts can learn as much as we can about ourselves so that we can be effective instruments for our patients. But Freud could not be as specific as we can be in actually characterizing what we need to learn. We have learned, through years of clinical and introspective experience, that self esteem and relatedness are essential dimensions of human psychological experience, and that as analysts we need to manage our need for both in order to be open to the relational needs of our patients and allow for true engagement with them.

Thus, the attitude of "Openness" is predicated on our own self maintenance, and our ability to recognize and satisfy our own relational needs. This expands the domain of technique beyond the confines of the analytic hour, and into the zone where we are who we really are. This is important for us to talk and think about if we are to rise to the challenge implicit in thinking about the role of our unique personalities in analytic technique.

2. Remember The Transference

Back in the early days of analysis, Sterba wrote a seminal paper emphasizing

"...one of the most important processes in analytic therapy, namely, the effecting of a dissociation within the ego by interpretation of the patient's instinctually conditioned conduct and his defensive reaction to it. Perhaps I may say... that the therapeutic dissociation of the ego in analysis is merely an extension, into new fields, of that self-contemplation which from all time has been regarded as the most essential trait of man in distinction to other living beings." (Sterba, (1934, p. 125.).

While Sterba was speaking in the language of ego psychology, the attitude he was advocating transcends the terms particular to the structural theory, and is key to helping patients develop a perspective on their own subjective world through an appreciation of it's transference dimension. With all of our current emphasis on what is new and transformative in the analytic experience, it is easy to forget what is old.

Regardless of one's theoretical persuasion, analysis has something to do with the past as it lives in the present, and the benefits to be derived from distinguishing the two. It is the analyst's job to keep track of the transferential relevance of the emotional field at any particular moment, and to help the patient become aware of it through interpretation.

It may seem as if this is such a fundamental point that it goes without saying. But as psychoanalysis has evolved to it's present state, the transference implications of the analytic dialogue often recede into the background, especially with patients who present histories of early trauma that inclines us toward an attitude of "deficit repair." Following Ferenczi, we seem to have learned overall that such patients can be further traumatized by a strictly interpretive approach. That has been a central tenet of this paper. But at the same time, an awareness of the transference dimension is essential in psychoanalytic work, whether we interpret the transference or not. Transference, resistance and the influence of the Unconscious on mental life are what make psychoanalytic work psychoanalytic.

In order to keep the transference in mind, we need to be reflective as well as open, to be able to step backward as well as forward. The ability to shift perspectives—to let ourselves go and to reel ourselves back—is a fundamental and hard won skill that is at the core of analytic technique.

3. Be Bold in Entering Enactments

In his "Technique" papers, Freud described a posture that enabled him to do battle with his patient's transference desires as they collided with the "basic rule" of free association that he had assigned to the those who consciously had solicited his help. As we have come to see, there is nowhere the analyst can sit to avoid being swept up by the pressures of the patient's unconscious and his own, and visa versa. Hence, the focus on what we now call "enactments."

Varga (2010) and others have helped us understand the usefulness of viewing enactments as a form of "free association," a co-constructed relational text that offers us a point of entry into the unconscious life of our patients just as they bring us an inevitable encounter with our own unconscious life.

This expanded vision of the analytic field lends itself to another recommendation: as enactments are inevitable and invisibility is not an option, let yourself get swept away by them by simply being yourself.

I am not advocating a disregard for boundaries or a license to engage in a contemporary version of "wild analysis." What I am advocating is a relaxation of inhibitions that interfere with the authenticity fundamental to establishing good human relationships. This can be as frightening for analysts as it is for our patients. Once we jump into the water of transference and surrender to the emotional currents, how does we avoid getting flipped out of the boat? To translate the metaphor: how does one avoid wrecking the analysis?

Freud's original technique papers can help us here. When Freud recommends that the analyst be like the surgeon, who does his work with a dispassionate attitude, we should keep in mind that surgeons are not only dispassionate—they are bold. The very creation of the psychoanalytic situation was the bold expression of Freud's personality. But along with the boldness required to jump into the water comes the necessity of pulling away from the action and remembering the importance of holding up the mirror—not only to the patient, but to ourselves—and asking "what does it mean?"

4. Analysis Transcends the Room

If we allow ourselves to become emotionally in tune with our patients, we find that that they are with us outside of our sessions. It follows that much of what occurs in sessions is dependent on processing that takes place outside of them, and that an expanded view of technique might encompass a variety of activities that relate to what we do with the emotions stirred up in us by our patients. This demands a great deal of self analysis and emotional processing on our part, that must take place outside of sessions. We could look at this as a matter of keeping ourselves in tune, and as such it belongs in the domain of technique. This runs counter to the traditional wisdom that thoughts about patients reflect countertransference "problems" within the analyst, just as our current appreciation of "countertransference" is that it is not part of the problem, but part of the solution.

VI. Pitfalls

I believe the above recommendations distinguish the

psychoanalytic process from other psychotherapies. Along the way of implementation, there are two major types of errors that can corrupt efforts to implement an analytic technique as described above. The first are errors of INHIBITION: our tendency to hold ourselves back from engagement. The theory of abstinence has long served to support such a defensive posture on the part of analysts.

Equally problematic are errors of EXHIBITION, in which the analyst is unrestrained in his intrusion into the therapeutic arena in order to fulfill his own needs at the expense of his patient's. It seems likely that we have gone, as a group, to erring on this side of the equation in reaction to years of erring on the side of holding ourselves back.

What are correctives to these errors? It should go without saying that a respect for BOUNDARIES and a sense of ethics are essential analytic attitudes. But beyond that, our patients themselves are usually very forthright in their diagnosis of us, and who they need us to be (Hoffman, 1983). It seems to me that to withhold from a patient a "Corrective Emotional Experience" that we bring with us by virtue of being who we are and who we are not is an unnecessary albatross for us to hang upon our necks. To the extent that we authentically embody the attributes they require, why not be open in employing them on their behalf when we are able to do so?

There is an analogy here, if not an identity, to parenting. As our children get to know us, they tell us who we are and what they need from us using the means of communication at their disposal. Wise parents learn from this.

Last, but certainly not least, comes HUMILITY. Our ability to promote helpful change in our patients is significant, but limited. Such change is more likely to occur, paradoxically, if we are able to maintain a high degree of humility in our work, despite the grandiose ambitions we often bring with us to this career. And I've got to admit, it takes a fair amount of grandiosity to undertake a career in psychoanalysis, which Freud so aptly described as an impossible profession.

Our own grandiosity can interfere with the recognition of the grandiosity in our patients, which so often conceals vulnerability and hides where the hurt is, for both patient and analyst. An attitude of humility promotes the analytic task of trying to understand our patients within the limits of our capacities.

There is one more way in which an attitude of humility is useful. That has to do with our relationship with the different psychoanalytic theories that compete with each other for a place in our Institute Curricula. When we invite the unconscious into our consulting rooms, it is very tempting to imagine that we know what by definition isn't knowable. Theory may start us off, but thinking that "we know" can be an obstacle to empathy and its operation in the psychoanalytic process.

VII. Conclusions

I have tried in the paragraphs above to make the case that use of The Analyst's unique personality should be recognized as a fundamental aspect of technique, and that the relational elements, once recognized, are coequal in importance to the interpretative activity that is also fundamental to analysis. While the use of the analyst's personality encompasses so many responses as to make specific recommendations impossible, Roy Schafer's idea of "analytic attitude" is prescient and seems more important than ever as a way of teaching of students who want to learn how to use themselves as "analytic instruments" in the service of their patients. I believe the above recommendations distinguish the psychoanalytic process from other psychotherapies, and that they may be useful as a contemporary update to Freud's initial "Recommendations to Physicians Beginning Psychoanalysis".

References

Alexander, F. (1935). The Problem of Psychoanalytic Technique. *Psychoanal Q.,* 4:588–611.

——— (1950). Analysis of the Therapeutic Factors in Psychoanalytic Treatment. *Psychoanal Q.,* 19:482–500.

Bacal, H.A. (1990). The Elements of a Corrective Selfobject Experience. *Psychoanal. Inq.,* 10:347–372.

Boston Change Process Study Group (2013). Enactment and the Emergence of a New Relational Organization. *JAPA,* 61:727–749.

Ferenczi, S. (1949). Confusion of the Tongues Between the Adults and the Child. *Int. J. Psycho-Anal.,* 30:225–230.

———& Rank, O. (1925). *The Development of Psychoanalysis.* Washington, DC: Nervous and Mental Disease Publishing Co.

Freud, S. (1912). The dynamics of transference. *Standard Edition,* 12:97–108.

——— (1913). On beginning the treatment. (Further recommendations on the technique of psycho-analysis I.) *Standard Edition,* 12:121–144.

——— (1914). Remembering, repeating and working-through. (Further recommendations on the technique of psycho-analysis II.) *Standard Edition,* 12:145–156.

——— (1915). Observations on transference-love. *Standard Edition,* 12:157–171.

Friedman, L. (2008). A Renaissance for Freud's Papers on Technique. *Psychoanal Q.,* 77:1031–1044.

Lipton, S.D. (1977). The Advantages of Freud's Technique as Shown in his Analysis of the Rat Man. *Int. J. Psycho-Anal.,* 58:255–273.

Schafer, R (1983). *The Analytic Attitude.* New York: Basic Books.

Sterba, R. (1934). The Fate of the Ego in Analytic Therapy. *Int. J. Psycho-Anal.,* 15:117–126.

Varga, M.P. (2010). Integrating Classical and Relational Psychoanalysis: The Therapeutic Action of Analyst's and Patient's Interacting Transferences. *Psychoanal. Rev.,* 97:531–556.

Chapter 8
What Anonymity? A Response to the Problem with Psychoanalytic Anonymity: The Obstacles Created by the Persistence of Traditional Technique

Himanshu Agrawal

The year was 2010. I received an email on all of my email accounts—my personal accounts as well as my work email. *"Hi, this is _____, and I am _____'s son. She sees you in your clinic, and I really need to talk to you about her mental health. Sorry for contacting you this way but she wouldn't give me your phone number and I couldn't think of any other way."*

Later on, I found out he had paid $0.99 to an online service, and it had provided him with my divorce details and my home address in addition to my email addresses.

Later, in 2016, I discovered in a rather ugly fashion that any and all of one's photographs could be stolen from a prominent social media account without one's permission. Apparently, all you had to do was use a certain online service, type in someone's name and shell out $4.99.

What anonymity?

In his initial invitation for me to write to response to Dr. Henry Friedman's paper The *Problem with Psychoanalytic Anonymity: The Obstacles Created by the Persistence of Traditional Technique*, Dr. Neal Spira wrote "I know that you and Henry have had interactions over civility on the (American Psychoanalytic Association members) listserv— so I confess that having you comment has a perverse appeal to me." As I composed this response to Henry's paper, a part of me resisted Dr. Spira's implied desire, and a part of me submitted to it. I will leave it up to the reader to discover and decide where each part prevails within this commentary.

To start with, Friedman's paper is written in his characteristic style—easy to read and articulate. (I learned a new word— "dourness.") It is compelling on several occasions (e.g., when he writes "Once an analyst concludes that the basis for all our theories are indeed theoretical and unable to be either disproven or proven it is possible to face the need to be real with his patients. (sic)" What a lovely line! Dr. Friedman's piece begins as many psychoanalytic papers do—invoking Sigmund Freud. It introduces the reader to the origin story of psychoanalysis, psychoanalytic technique and the concept of the psychoanalyst's anonymity. I join Dr. Friedman in his critique when he asks why "Freud's theory has fared so poorly in much of the world where major modifications of his theory have prevailed." I believe one is correct to admonish the fanatical (and sometimes blind) servitude with which certain psychoanalysts follow the dictates of Freud Senior, turning a blind eye to the major change in the zeitgeist over the last century. In an abstract entitled "What would Freud do...today?" (2023), I speculate that Sigmund Freud would be the first one to chide us "modern" psychoanalysts for at least two reasons : (i) cherry-picking the techniques he developed (why don't graduate analysts return to psychoanalysis every few years like the master recommended?), and (ii) staying rigid and dogmatic to what he *said* a hundred years ago, rather than what he *did* across his lifetime, which was to revise his own theories innumerable times as he received new information about the world outside and inside of him. He himself completely revised his basic models of the mind on at least three different occasions—the Trauma Affect model (1894), then the Topographical model (1915) and finally the Structural model (1923). Who knows what his proposed techniques would have looked like in 2023 had he kept going!

I tend to agree with Friedman's implications that if a contemporary psychoanalyst insists on holding the concept of anonymity to a literal standard developed a century ago, they might be missing the forest for the trees.

Next, Dr. Friedman walks us through the major schools of psychoanalytic theory that evolved post Freud (starting with Freud's daughter and heir apparent, Anna). He uses select examples of several prominent figures from the annals of psychoanalysis (Klein, Bion, Kris, Brenner, Arlow to name a few) as he comments on how the concept of anonymity may have been influenced over the decades as additional thought-leaders broke out on to the psychoanalytic scene. Unfortunately, this is where Dr. Friedman somewhat loses me. To me, his narrative of the effects of post-Freud theorists does not quite feel like a balanced commentary about occurrences in psychoanalytic history. Instead, it feels a little bit like he may be picking and choosing parts of the Colossal psychoanalytic archives to bolster the (valid) points he wishes to make about how psychoanalysts have approached the concept of anonymity. I would argue that there are several arguments made in psychoanalytic literature that would agree with the points Henry is making in his essay. As I listen to myself writing this, even as I fantasize that Dr. Friedman is "cherry picking" literature, it strikes me whether that is the very point that was on Henry's mind when he wrote his paragraphs—that historically, as a community, psychoanalysts tend to cherry pick psychoanalytic literature to suit their practice styles (and there is so much to pick from, so one is likely to find what one is looking for, irrespective of where one's stance on, say, anonymity). If this is indeed what Friedman was helping us understand, then I would concur whole heartedly.

The next paragraph (which starts with "External reality was widely seen as irrelevant or even more likely the enemy of a true analysis."), I have to state, was my favorite! I find it to be a laser sharp dissection and criticism of how the psychoanalytic system has unfortunately used the concepts of neutrality and anonymity defensively, which I believe have ended up doing disservice to many of its stakeholders. Dr. Friedman describes with his signature confidence how the William Alanson White Institute was created, and of course, it would be important to enquire about the details from the William Alanson White Institute itself.

Having said that, I must confess I was somewhat confused when he stated "there is little to indicate where the relational school stands with regard to the important issue of self-disclosure on the analyst's part," since I believe a search on the Psychoanalytic Electronic Publishing archive (PEPWEB) will show the plethora of literature that could answer this question, for instance, the relational analysts' comfortability with self-disclosing (Knight, 2009), concerns about excessive self-disclosure (Aron, Grand & Slochower, 2018), and an entire chapter dedicated to the nuances of self-disclosure (Kuchuk, 2021) just for starters.

I would also submit that clubbing "anonymity, abstinence and neutrality" all in the same sentence and speak of these very complex (and very different concepts) as if they were interchangeable seems a bit unfair, especially if there are readers who are relatively new to our beloved field. I wonder if Friedman ends up using the term 'anonymity' in his essay when, perhaps, he meant to describe neutrality (e.g., when he states, "the analyst was placed in the position, not so much as he or she who knew the answers, but as a careful worker observing the associations moving in front of him, until some aspect of the unconscious could be spotted and called to the patient's attention.") or abstinence (e.g., when he writes "He did participate by his interpretations, but his feelings were to be seen as countertransference and, as such, needed to be contained, split off, for his own consideration but not to be shared with the patient.").

While I am in confession mode, please allow me to own up further—I found myself somewhat puzzled when Friedman wrote about "The power of psychoanalytic rules for technique" and asserted that "it has only been in psychoanalysis that such rules have been promulgated and maintained as established without any proof, experimentally *or clinically*, to prove their importance or their effectiveness," (emphasis added on bolded and italicized portion). One of the most compelling arguments for me to pursue a career in psychoanalysis came from the hundreds of clinical case presentations I have attended as case after case reveals the anecdotal evidence and importance of the effectiveness of these techniques! (Now, if Friedman implies that psychoanalysts need to work harder in accumulating experimental evidence, I agree with my colleague without any reservations.)

Friedman makes a fair point about how, in many psychoanalytic circles, self-disclosure has been seen as a slippery slope towards crossing sexual boundaries between analyst and analysand. I find this to be true especially if self-disclosure is used as part of seduction. Having said that, as someone who just read the author complaining about the lack of proof (when writing about the importance of psychoanalytic technique), I would have appreciated some references when Henry claims, "the majority of sexual romances between analyst and patient tended to be between a male analyst and a female candidate who was in analysis as part of her training."

Although it is interesting to hear a bit about Dr. Friedman's perspective on the local politics in Bostonian psychoanalytic circles, I am afraid I am unable to grasp how the section about the Training Analyst system is relevant to the topic of anonymity. Perhaps he wishes to educate us, using the Boston example, how a dogmatic, rigid adherence to tradition has

149

created obstacles in the world of psychoanalysis. Even if that is the case, I must say that in the example he uses, I may experience the outcome (the creation of an additional psychoanalytic institute) differently than what Henry implies—to me, the end results seems overall positive, creating a potential space for a diversity of opinions, techniques and options within our field—hardly an obstacle.

In closing, I will say that there is no doubt in my opinion that the rigid adherence to traditional psychoanalytic techniques (including the practice of anonymity in the same way as it was orchestrated in the early 1900s) may create obstacles in the delivery of modern psychoanalysis.

I look forward to Dr. Friedman's response to my response, and then my response to his response to my response, and so on and so forth…at least it's not on a national listserv (which should serve much more important purposes than to endure monologues, whether they be Henry's or mine!)

References

Agrawal, H (2023). "What Would Freud Do…today?"—assessing the effectiveness of a curriculum designed to introduce the modern psychiatry resident to Sigmund Freud, APsA 111th Annual Meeting, New York City, New York.

Aron, L., Grand, S., & Slochower, J.A. (2018b). *Decentering relational theory: A comparative critique*. New York, NY: Routledge.

Busch, F. (2020). Response to Friedman. *International Journal of Controversial Discussions,* 1(2):100–101.

Freud, S. (1894). The neuro psychoses of defence. *Standard Edition,* 3:41–61.

——— (1915). *The unconscious. Standard Edition,* 14:159–204.

——— (1923). *The ego and the id. Standard Edition,* 19:1–66.

Hoffman, I.Z. (1983). The Patient as Interpreter of the Analyst's Experience. *Contemporary Psychoanalysis*, 19:389–422.

Knight, Z.G. (2009). Conceptual Considerations regarding Self-Disclosure: A Relational Psychoanalytic Perspective. *South African Journal of Psychology*, 39(1):75–85. doi:10.1177/008124630903900106

Kuchuck, S. (2021). *The Relational Revolution in Psychoanalysis and Psychotherapy*, Chapter 3: Self Disclosure. Confer Books: London.

Chapter 9
Henry Friedman's Response to the Discussants

The opportunity to publish a psychoanalytic paper in which I was free to express critical ideas about how I believe psychoanalysis has been formulated and practiced over the past fifty years is one that I deeply appreciate because I know how rare it is. Only an online journal like this one *(International Journal of Controversial Discussions)* would permit me the opportunity to say what I think and believe to be true about problems with how psychoanalysis has been practiced without being told by the Journal's editor that what I said would need to be modified (often to the point of becoming a different paper) or the paper would never see the light of day. The ability to speak critically about psychoanalysis is a gift that Arnie Richards has offered psychoanalysis; it is rare gift particularly in the world of psychoanalysis where our Journals stand, often unconsciously but sometimes consciously, as the outlet for conservative voices that promote ideas that are acceptable to those who have the power to control the message that any Journal represents.

What I wrote in my paper was the result of what I had learned over many years of clinical practice during which I had to overcome the many rules that were promulgated during both my years of training and those that were to follow. I have always felt that what I was aiming at in the analyses that I participated in as psychoanalyst was a relationship with another individual who had been burdened by their life experience even if that burden allowed them to be successful or even famous in the life they were living. I felt a confidence in my way of relating to my patients that I knew was different from what I had been taught and what I observed with patients who had previously been in therapy or analysis with other psychoanalysts. My focus was on the ubiquitous influence of received wisdom about the role of the psychoanalyst and in particular on the need for a constrained, rather under reactive individual, who lived in a world of interpretations of their patients unconscious motivations.

I am pleased to see that several of my colleagues have responded to my paper by writing their own papers. Some of these begin with a consideration of my critical perspective but then abruptly turn in another direction as if to indicate either an unwillingness to address my objections to classical technique or a desire to go in another direction all together. What I found in their responses varied from connected and additive to my position or disconnected and dismissive without actually stating that to be the case. Of course, I appreciate each of their responses and the time it took to read and reflect on my paper. I remember hearing Owen Renik, at one of our national meetings, proclaim that to be good at either psychoanalysis or love making you needed to be relaxed. I think his message is somehow incorporated into my paper simply because asking another individual to say everything about their thoughts while you, as analyst, responded with interpretations, seemed to require a kind of uptightness that was artificial and off putting as an experience for both the patient and the analyst. I do notice how often my colleagues like to believe that what I write about openness and self-disclosure is unnecessary because we have progressed to a point where we all have given up the rules. This I continue to doubt and question. New analytic theories and schools seem never to address the issue of technique. The old, and antiquated technical requirements persist and keep their hold on clinicians. The Prison House of Psychoanalysis may have been Arnold Goldberg's choice of a title that didn't mean it in the way that I do. Well intentioned psychoanalysts who continue to protect their identity from their patients may have excellent results but that fails to convince me that anonymity, neutrality and abstinence aren't techniques that make the achievement of therapeutic effectiveness more difficult to achieve.

If this volume and my paper can help those who read it reconsider where they stand with regard to the issue of psychoanalytic technique then it will feel like writing the paper and reading my colleagues responses and responding to them has been a worthy use of my time. I hope that those who read my paper and those that follow it will feel similarly that their time has been well spent. It is my belief that psychoanalysts need to work with more inclusion of their true self rather than a professionalized version of who they are that is deemed as necessary for what they do with patients qualify as psychoanalysis.

Historically, we as psychoanalysts have devoted too much energy to protecting the purity of psychoanalysis. This has been particularly true when it comes to issues of technique, much more than has been the case with theory. Many theories have been found acceptable despite their challenges to Freud's basic ideas; they have co-existed and utilized by individual psychoanalysts without regard for contradictions between the theories they are using. I have chosen to challenge the seeming immutability of classical technique, starting with anonymity. For me, this is an important project if for no other reason than patients are often put off by it and seek out other therapists who are free of the stigma of classical Freudian psychoanalytic technique.

Concluding Remarks by Neal Spira

Thanks to Henry Friedman for providing us this opportunity to weigh in on psychoanalytic technique at this moment in the history of our discipline. Indeed, this seems to be one of those moments in the evolution of our field where theory, practice, and advancements in neuroscience call for this kind of self-examination.

There seems to be little disagreement among our contributors that technique derived from classical theory does not necessarily help patients get better, sometimes interferes with their getting better, and sometimes makes patients worse. Experience teaches us that healing often requires "something else" provided within the patient-analyst relationship. The importance of that "something else" can't be overestimated. Dr. Friedman make a good argument that traditional psychoanalytic theory and technique potentially blind us to the two-person nature of "where the action is" in therapy. Then there is the problem of the incompatibility of traditional psychoanalytic theory and technique with what we have discovered about how the brain operates.

In that regard, if Dr. Friedman's essay is read as an invitation to re-examine our old concepts, it's a most welcome one. If read as an argument to retire concepts like transference, resistance and the unconscious—it becomes even more interesting.

At a similar moment in time, when oedipally oriented ego psychology was being challenged by the emergence of object relations theory and self psychology, Hans Loewald wrote "The Waning of the Oedipus Complex" (Loewald, H. W. 1979 The Waning of the Oedipus Complex. *Journal of the American Psychoanalytic Association* 27:751–775). Loewald had two aims: 1) to re-revaluate the Oedipus in terms of newer understandings; and 2) to address the psychoanalytic community's relationship to the emergence of new ideas. Regarding the second:

"Our hitherto normal form of organizing reality, aiming at a strict distinction and separation between an internal, subjective, and an external, objective world, is in question. Our psychotic core, as it comes increasingly into view, prevents us from being as much at home and at ease with this solution as our scientific forefathers were. I believe that our quest for individuation and individuality, and for an objective world view, is being modulated by insights we are gaining from the 'psychic reality' of preoedipal life stages. We even need to reexamine Freud's distinction between psychic reality and factual, objective reality. Not that this distinction might be invalid. But its validity appears to be more circumscribed and limited than we assumed, analogous to Newtonian physics: the new theories and discoveries of modern physics do not invalidate Newtonian physics, but they limit its applicability.

Interest in the Oedipus complex has been on the wane because of these developments. But it is also true that perspectives on the Oedipus complex are changing, that the different modes of its waning and waxing during life stages give it renewed significance and weight, and that the intermediate nature of incestuous relations, intermediate between identification and object cathexis, throws additional light on its centrality. I have pointed out that the superego as the heir of the Oedipus complex is the structure resulting from parricide, representing both guilt and atonement for the usurpation of authority. We are reminded that the oedipal attachments, struggles, and conflicts must also be understood as new versions of the basic union-individuation dilemma. The superego, as the culmination of individual psychic structure formation, represents something ultimate in the basic separation-individuation process" (Loewald, p. 774).

If we attempt to assimilate Dr. Friedman's essay and the contributions of our discussants into this framework, we can appreciate that the struggle to liberate ourselves from our predecessors involves (at least within the theory we are killing off) the act of "theoretical" parricide. And yet it's largely through our failed attempts to apply "classical" theory that we've arrived at a place where we can recognize its limitations and new territory. The degree to which this process—which is a process of growth—will lead to retirement/rejection/repression vs internalization/atonement is not yet known, a work in progress, and our story to tell.

How shall we tell it? One way, as Bhaskar Sripada suggests, is to hold ourselves to the task of describing our own inner experiences and the way they emerge in our contributions to the two person psychoanalytic process. In other words, being as "real" as we can be in our accounts of our clinical interactions. But in the analytic moment, and the series of moments that constitutes the analytic relationship, there is the lingering question of what it means for the analyst to be real.

There are other questions, as well. What words do we use to talk about the real relationship? Do we need a new conceptual language to free ourselves from the vestiges of terms derived from a one-person psychology? Can the "real relationship" exist without reference to its one-person opposite? Last but not least—do efforts to analyze the elements of give and take destroy the spontaneous essence of what is real in the real relationship?

There is, clearly, much work to be said and done, and I appreciate having had the opportunity to help set the stage for this discussion of a matter so important to our intrinsically controversial field.

———————————

About the Contributors

Himanshu Agrawal, M.D., DFAPA

was born in New Delhi and spent his childhood living with his family in Bangladesh, London, Moscow, and Nepal. Himanshu emigrated to USA in 2002 to pursue training in child psychiatry. He is a newly minted psychoanalyst and was Minnesota Psychoanalytic Institute's first-ever long-distance candidate. Over half of Himanshu's personal/training analysis has been conducted long distance. He has served on APsA's board of directors, and as the president of the APsA candidates' council. He is the editor of the book *'Dear Institute...'* (which is a global commentary on psychoanalytic training).

Himanshu lives in Milwaukee, and as an associate professor of psychiatry and behavioral medicine at the Medical College of Wisconsin, he sees patients, conducts research, and teaches psychotherapists, pharmacy students, medical students, advance practice providers and physicians. He enjoys a wide array of topics, however his area of academic interest lies in psychodynamic psychiatry, psychoanalysis, wellbeing, burnout and stigma.

Lance Dodes, M.D. is a Training and

Supervising Analyst Emeritus at the Boston Psychoanalytic Society and Institute, member of the faculty of the New Center for Psychoanalysis (Los Angeles) and retired assistant clinical professor of psychiatry at Harvard Medical School. He is the author or senior author of many journal articles and book chapters about the psychology of compulsive and addictive behavior, and author of three books on the topic. He contributed the chapter "Sociopathy" to the recent

bestselling book, *The Dangerous Case of Donald Trump*. He currently lives in Los Angeles where he and his wife moved from Boston to be near their grandchildren.

Henry J. Friedman, M.D. is a psychiatrist and psychoanalyst who trained in medicine at the Johns Hopkins school of medicine and at the Harvard Medical School program in psychiatry. He has been in the private practice of psychoanalysis and analytic psychotherapy since 1980 and has been an associate professor of psychiatry at both Tufts and Harvard Medical Schools. His main focus has been on the need for critical reappraisal of both psychoanalytic theory and technique. He is particularly concerned about incompatibilities involved in different psychoanalytic theories and the failure to question some of the basic assumptions of psychoanalysis that have been treated as received wisdoms, not to be questioned. He has reviewed over 70 psychoanalytic books from an independent critical perspective.

Dale Gody, Ph.D., FABP, is a faculty member and Training and Supervising Analyst at the Chicago Psychoanalytic Institute. She teaches relational theory, psychoanalysis and feminism, and case report writing. Currently she resides in Salt Lake City where she maintains a practice of adult psychotherapy and psychoanalysis and couples therapy.

Edward Nersessian, M.D., Clinical Professor of Psychiatry, Weil Cornell Medical School. Training and Supervising Psychoanalyst, New York Psychoanalytic Institute/Society Director, The Helix Center for Multidisciplinary Studies.

Deana Schuplin, LMHC, FABP has been immersed in clinical work since 1982. She completed a psychoanalytic psychotherapy program at the Cleveland Psychoanalytic Center in the late 1990's. In 2005 she entered psychoanalytic training there before transferring to the Greater Kansas City Psychoanalytic Institute in 2006 when she moved with her husband for a job opportunity to Des Moines, Iowa.

Ms. Schuplin completed psychoanalytic training in 2012, became nationally certified in adult psychoanalysis in 2017 and was appointed as a Training and Supervising Analyst by the GKCPI in 2020. She has a private practice in Des Moines, Iowa.

Neal Spira, M.D. is a psychiatrist, psychoanalyst and Director at Large for APsaA. He is past president of the Chicago Psychoanalytic Society and a former Dean of the Chicago Psychoanalytic Institute, where he is currently a training and supervising analyst. Dr. Spira has written on a variety of applied psychoanalytic topics including the way psychoanalysis interfaces with religion, politics and public health. He currently writes a blog "Understanding Backwards" on the Substack platform.

Bhaskar Sripada, M.D., a practicing psychoanalyst since 1980 and a faculty member at the Chicago Institute for Psychoanalysis since 1995, resides and practices in Chicago. He has authored several psychoanalytic papers and a memoir, *When Suicide Beckons,* which details his countertransference experience treating a depressed patient. Along with many contemporary analysts, he believes that both the patient and analyst are active participant observers and, therefore, in this book, he provides details of the ongoing transference-countertransference of the analytic process. Accordingly, he has detailed the ongoing emotions, thoughts, childhood memories, life experiences, and analytic training that shaped his technique and responsiveness to the patient, thus helping the reader appreciate the complexity and depth of psychoanalytic treatment.

www.ingramcontent.com/pod-product-compliance
Lightning Source LLC
Chambersburg PA
CBHW060230030426
42335CB00014B/1388